Whaddaya Say?

Guided Practice in Relaxed Speech

NINA WEINSTEIN

Longman

Dedication

I dedicate this book to my husband, David, and son, Joshua, for being patient with my busy schedule and understanding why this book is so important.

Whaddaya Say? Guided Practice in Relaxed Speech, Second Edition

Copyright © 2001, 1982 by Prentice Hall Regents
Addison Wesley Longman, Inc.
A Pearson Education Company.

Pearson Education, 10 Bank Street, White Plains, NY 10606

Vice president, director of publishing: Allen Ascher
Editorial director: Louisa Hellegers
Acquisitions editor: Eleanor Kirby Barnes
Senior development manager: Penny Laporte
Development editor: Paula Van Ells
Vice president, director of design and production: Rhea Banker
Executive managing editor: Linda Moser
Production manager: Ray Keating
Associate production editor: Melissa Leyva
Director of Manufacturing: Patrice Fraccio
Senior manufacturing buyer: Edith Pullman
Cover design: Ann France
Text design: Patricia Woszczyk
Text composition: Carlisle Communications
Text art: Don Robb, Penny Carter

Library of Congress Cataloging-in-Publication Data

Weinstein, Nina J.
    Whaddaya say? Guided Practice in Relaxed Speech / Nina Weinstein.—2nd ed. p. cm.
    ISBN 0-201-67040-2
      1. English language—Textbooks for foreign speakers.   2. English language—Spoken English—Problems, exercises, etc.   3. English language—Idioms—Problems, exercises, etc.
I. Title.

PE1128 .W4264 2000
428.3'4—dc21

00-051447

10 11 12 13 14–BB–12 11 10 09

Contents

Introduction

Whaddaya Say? Second Edition is the result of twenty-five years of research on reduced forms. It's an updated, easy-to-use listening book that teaches the most common reduced forms (*wanna, *gonna, *gotta, etc.) needed to understand natural spoken English. *Whaddaya Say?* presents each reduced form fully contextualized in practical, fun conversations.

Reduced forms are the pronunciation changes that occur in natural speech because of the environment or context in which a word or sound is found. The amount of reduction (the level) depends on how fast the word or sound is spoken.

Example:

SLOW SPEECH	FASTER	FASTEST
Level 1: *want to*	Level 2: *want *ta*	Level 3: *wanna*

Whaddaya Say? focuses on Level 3 reduced forms because, according to research, this level is the most common. A detailed list of reductions that have three or more levels is included on page 119.

DESIGN OF THE CHAPTERS

Whaddaya Say? Second Edition includes updated versions of the original twenty chapters, plus ten new chapters on additional reductions. Each lesson follows the same chapter outline given below. There's also a review test section (Test Yourself) at the back of the book. The review tests are intended for students to use as both additional practice and a self-check. They concentrate on reduced forms that are often confused with each other. All of the chapters and tests appear on the accompanying audio program. As a general rule, each chapter represents about fifty minutes of presentation and practice material.

Part 1: Introduction
CONVERSATION

In the conversations, students are introduced to the reduced forms for that lesson. After Chapter 1, previously learned forms are recycled in the conversations and throughout the chapters.

Students first listen to a segment of a conversation spoken with careful, slow pronunciation. They contrast this pronunciation with the same segment spoken with relaxed, fast speech that uses the target reduced forms. Afterward, the entire conversation is repeated using only relaxed, fast speech. Depending on their abilities, the students can follow along in their books or listen without looking at their books.

To remind students that the reduced forms are not to be used for written English, an asterisk (*) is used with every reduced form.

COMPREHENSION

The Comprehension questions check students' basic understanding of the conversation. Some questions ask the students to form opinions. Students can compare answers with a partner at the end of the exercise, and then share their answers with the class.

PRACTICE

Student books should be closed for the Practice section. This is basically a translation exercise in which students repeat only the slow, careful pronunciation of the relaxed, fast speech they hear. If students have difficulty, they can stop the tape recorder after each sentence to allow them to "translate" it in smaller, easier chunks.

Part 2: Expansion

COMPREHENSION

In this part, students hear a new conversation, usually a continuation of the opening conversation, but spoken in relaxed, fast pronunciation. The Comprehension questions can be used to ensure that students understand the key points of the second conversation. If students have difficulty answering these questions, they can listen to the audio program again. If students have difficulty understanding this conversation on the audio program, they can open their books to the Part 2 Practice section and follow along.

PRACTICE

In this section, students listen to the Part 2 conversation again, filling in the blanks with the missing reduced forms. They should use the conventional spellings of the reduced forms that they hear. For example, if they hear *'n', they should write *and*. After students have filled in all of the blanks, they listen again and check their answers before sharing the correct answers as a class.

DISCUSSION

Students can work in small groups to discuss the final questions on the chapter topic. The purpose of this section is to encourage students to bring their own experiences into the classroom and into their discussion of the chapter topic.

TEST YOURSELF

Ten review tests for easily confused reduced forms appear at the back of the book and at the end of the audio program. Each test consists of a short conversation featuring the target reduced forms. Students should take each test after they finish the chapter that appears next to it. If students have difficulty with a particular test, they should re-do the chapters with the reduced forms that caused the difficulty. Students can also do the entire Test Yourself when they finish *Whaddaya Say?* to reinforce their understanding of relaxed speech.

An Answer Key for each Part 2, Practice and Test Yourself is provided at the back of the book.

ACKNOWLEDGMENTS

I'd like to thank my development editor, Megan Webster, for her careful comments, and the wonderful production staff for their detailed work. Penny Laporte is an incomparable joy to work with, and her important comments certainly focused the material. Louisa Hellegers and Eleanor Barnes were very helpful and insightful at every turn.

I'd especially like to thank all of my students at Toyota Motor Sales who helped to field-test *Whaddaya Say? Second Edition,* and the teachers and students I've met all over the world for sharing their success stories while using *Whaddaya Say?*

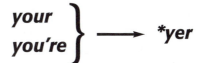

How's Your Family?

> your
> you're } ⟶ *yer
>
> Your and you're aren't pronounced *yer if stressed.

Part 1 INTRODUCTION

CONVERSATION

Listen to each part of the conversation: first spoken with careful (slow) pronunciation; then spoken with relaxed (fast) pronunciation.

Careful (Slow) Pronunciation	Relaxed (Fast) Pronunciation
CARLOS: Maria? Maria Gonzalez? My gosh! You're so tall now.	CARLOS: Maria? Maria Gonzalez? My gosh! *Yer so tall now.
MARIA: Carlos! My old neighbor! Wow! You're looking great.	MARIA: Carlos! My old neighbor! Wow! *Yer looking great.
CARLOS: Thanks. So . . . how's your family?	CARLOS: Thanks. So . . . how's *yer family?
MARIA: They're fine. How about *your* family?	MARIA: They're fine. How about *your* family?
CARLOS: They're fine, too.	CARLOS: They're fine, too.
MARIA: That's good. Does your mother still volunteer at a school?	MARIA: That's good. Does *yer mother still volunteer at a school?
CARLOS: Yes, she does.	CARLOS: Yes, she does.
MARIA: That's great. Your mother's a really nice person.	MARIA: That's great. *Yer mother's a really nice person.
CARLOS: You're right. She is. So, does your father still sing with his friends?	CARLOS: *Yer right. She is. So, does *yer father still sing with his friends?
MARIA: Every weekend.	MARIA: Every weekend.

Listen to the entire conversation again, spoken with relaxed (fast) pronunciation.

COMPREHENSION

Answer these questions about the conversation.

1. What's the relationship between Maria and Carlos?
2. How often do you think they see each other? Explain.
3. What do you know about each family?
4. What do you think Carlos' mother does at the school?
5. Where do you think Maria's father sings every weekend?

Now, work with a partner and compare your answers.

PRACTICE

Close your book. You'll hear each part of the conversation spoken with relaxed pronunciation. Repeat each part using careful pronunciation.

Part 2 EXPANSION

COMPREHENSION

Listen to the conversation. The speakers use relaxed pronunciation.
Answer the questions.

1. Which family moved? When?
2. What do you know about Carlos' sister and Maria's brother?
3. Which family members don't know about the marriage plans?
4. Why do you think some family members don't know?
5. Do you think Carlos wants his sister to marry Maria's brother? Explain.
6. Should Carlos and Maria tell their parents about the marriage plans? Explain.
7. The best title for this conversation is
   a. Good Friends   b. An Exciting Marriage   c. Invite Me to the Divorce   d. Other _____

Work with a partner. Compare your answers. Listen again if necessary.

PRACTICE

Listen again. The conversation is spoken with relaxed pronunciation. Complete the sentences with the words you would hear if they were spoken with careful pronunciation. Then, listen once more and check your answers.

MARIA: Carlos, _____ family moved two years ago, right?
1

CARLOS: Yes.

MARIA: _____ twenty now?
2

CARLOS: Yes. And _____ seventeen?
3

MARIA: No. Eighteen.

CARLOS: Oh. _____ a mechanic now, right?
4

MARIA: That's right. So . . . _____ sister is a doctor in the Peace Corps, isn't she?
5

CARLOS: Uh huh.

MARIA: Is she still in India?

CARLOS: Yes. She loves India. Is _____ brother still an actor in Hollywood?
6

MARIA: Yeah. He does a soap commercial on TV. He e-mails _____ sister
7

every day.

CARLOS: Do _____ parents know they plan to get married?
8

MARIA: No. Do _____ parents know?
9

CARLOS: I don't think so. _____ brother and my sister have really different
10

lives.

MARIA: _____ not happy about their engagement?
11

CARLOS: I'm just worried. They're so different.

MARIA: _____ right. They are.
12

DISCUSSION

Work in small groups.

Is it better for a husband and wife to be interested in the same things? Explain.

2 Yours Is a Great Job!

yours ⟶ **yers*

Part 1 INTRODUCTION

CONVERSATION

Listen to each part of the conversation: first spoken with careful (slow) pronunciation; then spoken with relaxed (fast) pronunciation.

Careful (Slow) Pronunciation	Relaxed (Fast) Pronunciation
LINDA: I just got a raise at work.	LINDA: I just got a raise at work.
TIM: Really? I love your job.	TIM: Really? I love *yer job.
LINDA: I love yours.	LINDA: I love *yers.
TIM: Your job pays really well.	TIM: *Yer job pays really well.
LINDA: Yours is interesting.	LINDA: *Yers is interesting.
TIM: Your boss teaches the employees new things.	TIM: *Yer boss teaches the employees new things.
LINDA: But yours is funny.	LINDA: But *yers is funny.
TIM: You're right, but your job is near your home.	TIM: *Yer right, but *yer job is near *yer home.
LINDA: Yours is near your father-in-law's house.	LINDA: *Yers is near *yer father-in-law's house.
TIM: Yeah. Yours is far from my father-in-law's house . . . I love your job.	TIM: Yeah. *Yers is far from my father-in-law's house . . . I love *yer job.

Listen to the entire conversation again, spoken with relaxed (fast) pronunciation.

COMPREHENSION

Answer these questions about the conversation.

1. Who got a raise?
2. What do you know about Linda's job?

3. What do you know about Tim's job?
4. Do you think Tim likes his father-in-law? Explain.

Now, work with a partner and compare your answers.

PRACTICE

Close your book. You'll hear each part of the conversation spoken with relaxed pronunciation. Repeat each part using careful pronunciation.

Part 2 EXPANSION

COMPREHENSION

Listen to the conversation. The speakers use relaxed pronunciation. Answer the questions.

1. What's Tim's problem?
2. How do you think he feels about the problem?
3. What does Linda like about Tim's job?
4. What does Tim like about Linda's job?
5. Guess what Tim's job is. Explain.
6. Guess what Linda's job is. Explain.

Work with a partner. Compare your answers. Listen again if necessary.

PRACTICE

Listen again. The conversation is spoken with relaxed pronunciation. Complete the sentences with the words you would hear if they were spoken with careful pronunciation. Then, listen once more and check your answers.

TIM: I didn't get a raise.

LINDA: Oh, Tim. I'm really sorry. But _____ is a great job.
                                              1

TIM: It doesn't pay very well.

LINDA: _____ job helps people. That's important.
                    2

TIM: _____ right, but _____ pays well.
              3   4

LINDA: Money isn't everything. _____ co-workers are nice.
                                            5

TIM: _____ are really intelligent.
              6

LINDA: So are _____ .
                        7

TIM: _____ job is fun.
              8

LINDA: _____ isn't fun?
                9

TIM: Yeah, _____ right. _____ pays better, but my job is really fun.
                      10   11

DISCUSSION

Work in small groups.

Which is more important in a job—to make good money, to help people, or to have fun? Explain.

3 I Have the Perfect Car for You

> **for ——→ *fer**
>
> **For** doesn't become ***fer** if stressed or if it's not followed by another word. EXAMPLE: Who's this *for*?

Part 1 INTRODUCTION

CONVERSATION

Listen to each part of the conversation: first spoken with careful (slow) pronunciation; then spoken with relaxed (fast) pronunciation.

Careful (Slow) Pronunciation	Relaxed (Fast) Pronunciation

Careful (Slow) Pronunciation

JOHN: I'm looking for a car.

SALESPERSON: Okay. For a new car?

JOHN: No. For a used car.

SALESPERSON: For a recent model?

JOHN: Yes. For a late model economy car.

SALESPERSON: What price do you have in mind for the car?

JOHN: Around $8,500. What's your price range for economy cars?

SALESPERSON: You can't buy a late model for $8,500.

JOHN: You're sure?

SALESPERSON: Yes, sir. But I have a very nice late model for $11,900.

Relaxed (Fast) Pronunciation

JOHN: I'm looking *fer a car.

SALESPERSON: Okay. *Fer a new car?

JOHN: No. *Fer a used car.

SALESPERSON: *Fer a recent model?

JOHN: Yes. *Fer a late model economy car.

SALESPERSON: What price do you have in mind *fer the car?

JOHN: Around $8,500. What's *yer price range *fer economy cars?

SALESPERSON: You can't buy a late model *fer $8,500.

JOHN: *Yer sure?

SALESPERSON: Yes, sir. But I have a very nice late model *fer $11,900.

Listen to the entire conversation again, spoken with relaxed (fast) pronunciation.

COMPREHENSION

Answer these questions about the conversation.

1. What kind of car is John looking for?
2. How much does he want to spend?
3. Do you think this is enough money to buy a late model car? Explain.
4. Does the salesperson think this is enough money? Explain.
5. What does the salesperson offer John?
6. What do you think John will say next?

Now, work with a partner and compare your answers.

PRACTICE

Close your book. You'll hear each part of the conversation spoken with relaxed pronunciation. Repeat each part using careful pronunciation.

Part 2 EXPANSION

COMPREHENSION

Listen to the conversation. The speakers use relaxed pronunciation. Answer the questions.

1. Is John happy when he sees the car? Explain.
2. What does the salesperson say about each problem with the car?
3. What would John have to do to fix the car?
4. Would you buy a car from this salesperson? Why or why not?

Work with a partner. Compare your answers. Listen again if necessary.

PRACTICE

Listen again. The conversation is spoken with relaxed pronunciation. Complete the sentences with the words you would hear if they were spoken with careful pronunciation. Then, listen once more and check your answers.

SALESPERSON: Looking _____ 1 a car, sir?

JOHN: Yes. _____ 2 a used car.

SALESPERSON: _____ 3 a used car? _____ 4 in the right place.

JOHN: A late model economy car _____ 5 city driving. It's

_____ 6 my family.

SALESPERSON: Say no more. I have the perfect car _____ 7 city

driving. _____ 8 family will love it. Follow me.

JOHN: Is *this* it?

SALESPERSON: This is the one. Isn't it beautiful?

JOHN: But the paint's chipped.

SALESPERSON: No problem. _____ 9 a few extra dollars, we'll fix

that _____ 10 you. It'll look just like new.

JOHN: How many miles has it got?

SALESPERSON: Oh, around 95,000. But _____ 11 a few extra dollars,

we'll rebuild the engine. It'll be just like new.

JOHN: The tires are bald.

SALESPERSON: _____ 12 right. But _____ 13 a few more dollars, we'll

put on new tires. This will be a beautiful car _____ 14 _____ 15 family.

DISCUSSION

Work in small groups.

Compare this salesperson to salespeople you've met.

4 Where Are the Bags of Chips?

of ──────⟶ ***a***	

Of doesn't become ***a*** if stressed, or if it's not followed by another word. **EXAMPLE:**

A: Is it 3:00?
B: No. It's ten *of*.

Part 1 INTRODUCTION

CONVERSATION

Listen to each part of the conversation: first spoken with careful (slow) pronunciation; then spoken with relaxed (fast) pronunciation.

Careful (Slow) Pronunciation	Relaxed (Fast) Pronunciation
JULIE: The party's tonight. I've invited a lot of people.	JULIE: The party's tonight. I've invited a lot *a people.
SHOKO: Then, let's go shopping. It's already a quarter of three.	SHOKO: Then, let's go shopping. It's already a quarter *a three.
JULIE: You're right. It's late. Let's make a list.	JULIE: *Yer right. It's late. Let's make a list.
SHOKO: Okay. We need a case of soda.	SHOKO: Okay. We need a case *a soda.
JULIE: Right. We also need a bag of pretzels.	JULIE: Right. We also need a bag *a pretzels.
SHOKO: What about a few bags of chips?	SHOKO: What about a few bags *a chips?
JULIE: Okay. And a couple of packages of cheese for the dip.	JULIE: Okay. And a couple *a packages *a cheese *fer the dip.
SHOKO: Great. Your cheese dips are always so good.	SHOKO: Great. *Yer cheese dips are always so good.
JULIE: Thanks. We need a couple of other things, too.	JULIE: Thanks. We need a couple *a other things, too.
SHOKO: Wait. I don't have my credit card. Do you have yours?	SHOKO: Wait. I don't have my credit card. Do you have *yers?

Listen to the entire conversation again, spoken with relaxed (fast) pronunciation.

COMPREHENSION

Answer these questions about the conversation.

1. What are Julie and Shoko planning to do? When?
2. What do you think their relationship is?
3. How much cheese will they buy?
4. What other food do they need?
5. Who will pay for the food? Why?
6. Do you think they planned well for the party? Explain.

Now, work with a partner and compare your answers.

PRACTICE

Close your book. You'll hear each part of the conversation spoken with relaxed pronunciation. Repeat each part using careful pronunciation.

Part 2 EXPANSION

COMPREHENSION

Listen to the conversation. The speakers use relaxed pronunciation.
Answer the questions.

1. What food does Julie buy?
2. In which aisles does she find each kind of food?
3. Do you think Julie's party food is nutritious? Explain.
4. What party food would be more nutritious?
5. What time is the party?
6. What does Julie need to do before the party?

Work with a partner. Compare your answers. Listen again if necessary.

PRACTICE

Listen again. The conversation is spoken with relaxed pronunciation. Complete the sentences with the words you would hear if they were spoken with careful pronunciation. Then, listen once more and check your answers.

JULIE: Excuse me. Where's the milk?

CHECKER: It's down aisle 15.

JULIE: Thanks.

CHECKER: Excuse me, Miss. _____ going the wrong way. Aisle

                               1

15 is on _____ left.

          2

JULIE: Oh! Thank you. *(to herself)* I need three cartons _____

                                             3

milk and a few cartons _____ orange juice.

                          4

(to clerk) Excuse me. Where are the boxes _____ cookies?

                                               5

CLERK: Go down aisle 10. They're at the end _____ the aisle.

                                          6

They're beside the cans _____ nuts.

                          7

JULIE: Thanks. Oh! I also want meat _____ hamburgers.

                                    8

Where's the meat section?

CLERK: It's at the end _____ aisle 1. Aisle 1 is on _____

                            9   10

right, in the corner _____ the store.

                           11

JULIE: One more thing. I need buns _____ the hamburgers.

                                  12

CLERK: Hamburger buns are at the end _____ aisle 2, near the crackers.

                                          13

JULIE: Thank you. *(to another shopper)* Excuse me. What time is it?

SHOPPER: It's ten _____ four.

                        14

JULIE: *(to herself)* Oh, my gosh! I need to make all _____ the food _____

                                                 15   16

the party in two hours!

DISCUSSION

Work in small groups.

What food do you usually have at parties? Discuss.

5 Do You Like the Internet?

you ⟶ *ya

You isn't pronounced *ya* if stressed.

Part 1 INTRODUCTION

CONVERSATION

Listen to each part of the conversation: first spoken with careful (slow) pronunciation; then spoken with relaxed (fast) pronunciation.

Careful (Slow) Pronunciation	Relaxed (Fast) Pronunciation
JOSH: Grandpa, do you like the Internet?	JOSH: Grandpa, do *ya like the Internet?
GRANDPA: No. You can't do anything on the Internet.	GRANDPA: No. *Ya can't do anything on the Internet.
JOSH: Do you know how to use the Internet?	JOSH: Do *ya know how to use the Internet?
GRANDPA: Well, no. Do *you?*	GRANDPA: Well, no. Do *you?*
JOSH: Sure. I'll show you.	JOSH: Sure. I'll show *ya.
GRANDPA: No, thanks. The Internet's for young people.	GRANDPA: No, thanks. The Internet's *fer young people.
JOSH: The Internet's for everybody.	JOSH: The Internet's *fer everybody.
GRANDPA: Okay. How do you use the Internet?	GRANDPA: Okay. How do *ya use the Internet?
JOSH: Well, first, you find your Internet software on your computer screen.	JOSH: Well, first, *ya find *yer Internet software on *yer computer screen.
GRANDPA: Internet software? What are you talking about?	GRANDPA: Internet software? What are *ya talking about?

Listen to the entire conversation again, spoken with relaxed (fast) pronunciation.

COMPREHENSION

Answer these questions about the conversation.

1. How old do you think Josh's grandfather is? Why?
2. How old do you think Josh is? Why?
3. Do you think his grandfather has used a computer before? Explain.
4. Is his grandfather interested in the Internet? Explain.

Now, work with a partner and compare your answers.

PRACTICE

Close your book. You'll hear each part of the conversation spoken with relaxed pronunciation. Repeat each part using careful pronunciation.

Part 2 EXPANSION

COMPREHENSION

Listen to the conversation. The speakers use relaxed pronunciation.
Answer the questions.

1. Why doesn't Josh's grandfather want to find his movie on the Internet?
2. How do you get on the Internet?
3. Why does Josh's grandfather say, "You're almost ready to retire and buy a home in Florida"? Is he serious?
4. How does Josh's grandfather feel about the Internet by the end of the conversation?

Work with a partner. Compare your answers. Listen again if necessary.

PRACTICE

Listen again. The conversation is spoken with relaxed pronunciation. Complete the sentences with the words you would hear if they were spoken with careful pronunciation. Then, listen once more and check your answers.

GRANDPA: Let's do something fun today. Let's see Jackie Chan's new movie.

JOSH: Okay. Let me find _____ movie on the Internet.
                                          1

GRANDPA: Thanks, but that'll take _____ too long. I just want—
                                              2

JOSH: Look! There's Jackie Chan's latest movie! *Trading Kicks.*

GRANDPA: Wow! How do _____ do that so fast?
                                      3

JOSH: It's easy. First _____ open _____ Internet software
                                  4   5
like this. Then _____ type "Jackie Chan" here. That's all.
                            6

GRANDPA: _____ just a child, and _____ already know so much
                    7   8
about the Internet.

JOSH: Grandpa, I'm ten years old, _____ know!
                                              9

GRANDPA: Right. _____ ten years old. _____ almost ready to
                        10   11
retire and buy a home in Florida.

JOSH: Very funny, Grandpa.

GRANDPA: Look at this! The Internet gives _____ information about
                                                      12
all _____ Jackie Chan's movies!
            13

(Twenty minutes later)

JOSH: Grandpa, are _____ *still* on the Internet? When will
                              14
_____ be ready to leave _____ the movie?
        15   16

DISCUSSION

Work in small groups.

Do you know many elderly people who like the Internet? What do you think is the most interesting part of the Internet? Explain.

6 Let's Go Shopping

-ing endings ⟶ *-in'

Most native English speakers do not use the *-in' pronunciation for all -ing endings. The *-in' pronunciation is most often used with continuous verb tenses. The *-in' pronunciation is very informal.

Part 1 INTRODUCTION

CONVERSATION

Listen to each part of the conversation: first spoken with careful (slow) pronunciation; then spoken with relaxed (fast) pronunciation.

Careful (Slow) Pronunciation	Relaxed (Fast) Pronunciation

NANCY: Well, hi! You're shopping here, too!

KIM: Not really. I'm just looking around. So, how have you been?

NANCY: Great. I'm shopping with my sister. She's over there.

KIM: Is that your sister? The tall woman in front of the jackets?

NANCY: Yes. She's looking for a jacket for work.

KIM: Are you shopping for work clothes, too?

NANCY: No. I'm looking for a pair of jeans like yours.

KIM: Oh. I found these here last week for 30 percent off.

NANCY: For 30 percent off? Thanks for telling me.

KIM: Well, nice seeing you again. I hope you find what you're looking for.

NANCY: Well, hi! *Yer *shoppin' here, too!

KIM: Not really. I'm just *lookin' around. So, how have *ya been?

NANCY: Great. I'm *shoppin' with my sister. She's over there.

KIM: Is that *yer sister? The tall woman in front *a the jackets?

NANCY: Yes. She's *lookin' *fer a jacket *fer work.

KIM: Are *ya *shoppin' *fer work clothes, too?

NANCY: No. I'm *lookin' *fer a pair *a jeans like *yers.

KIM: Oh. I found these here last week *fer 30 percent off.

NANCY: *Fer 30 percent off? Thanks *fer *tellin' me.

KIM: Well, nice *seein' *ya again. I hope *ya find what *yer *lookin' for.

Listen to the entire conversation again, spoken with relaxed (fast) pronunciation.

COMPREHENSION

Answer these questions about the conversation.

1. What's Nancy doing?
2. How does Nancy greet Kim?
3. What are other ways to greet someone?
4. How well do you think Nancy and Kim know each other? Explain.
5. Why does Nancy thank Kim?
6. How does Kim say "good-bye"?
7. What are other ways to say "good-bye" in this situation?

Now, work with a partner and compare your answers.

PRACTICE

Close your book. You'll hear each part of the conversation spoken with relaxed pronunciation. Repeat each part using careful pronunciation.

Part 2 EXPANSION

COMPREHENSION

Listen to the conversation. The speakers use relaxed pronunciation. Answer the questions.

1. What kind of jeans does Nancy want?
2. Does Nancy know where the dressing room is at first? Explain.
3. How does she ask for more information about the dressing room?
4. What are other ways to ask for more information if you don't understand something?
5. Does Nancy like the fitted jeans? Explain.
6. Why does the salesperson suggest designer jeans?
7. What do you think Nancy will say next?

Work with a partner. Compare your answers. Listen again if necessary.

PRACTICE

Listen again. The conversation is spoken with relaxed pronunciation. Complete the sentences with the words you would hear if they were spoken with careful pronunciation. Then, listen once more and check your answers.

SALESPERSON: May I help _____ ?
                                  1

NANCY: Yes. I'm _____ _____ some jeans.
                          2   3

SALESPERSON: Are _____ _____ _____ fitted
                         4   5   6

    jeans, baggy jeans . . .

NANCY: Fitted jeans in a size 12.

SALESPERSON: We have two styles in _____ size. Here _____
                                 7   8

    are. Why don't _____ try them on in the dressing room over there?
                        9

NANCY: Excuse me. *Where's* the dressing room?

SALESPERSON: Over there. In the corner _____ the store, on
                                       10

    _____ right.
       11

(A few minutes later)

SALESPERSON: So, how were they?

NANCY: They were a little big, but that's okay. I'm really _____
                                             12

    _____ dressier jeans. _____ _____
       13   14   15

    to a play, _____ to a movie . . .
                   16

SALESPERSON: Dressy jeans . . . Well, _____ might be interested in
                                    17

    _____ a look at our designer jeans. A lot _____
       18   19

    people are _____ designer jeans _____ evening wear.
                    20   21

NANCY: Okay. Where are they?

SALESPERSON: Behind _____ . _____ _____ right
                          22   23   24

    in front _____ them.
              25

DISCUSSION

Work in small groups.

What do people you know wear to go out at night? Discuss.

7 What Are You Doing This Weekend?

> **What do you**
> **What are you** } ⟶ ***Whaddaya**
>
> A related form, ***Whadda,** is used when **What do** is followed by either *we* or *they*. EXAMPLES:
> ***Whadda** we need?
> ***Whadda** they want?

Part 1 INTRODUCTION

CONVERSATION

Listen to each part of the conversation: first spoken with careful (slow) pronunciation; then spoken with relaxed (fast) pronunciation.

Careful (Slow) Pronunciation	Relaxed (Fast) Pronunciation

KENJI: What are you doing this weekend?

TIM: Not much. What do you have in mind?

KENJI: Bungee jumping.

TIM: Bungee jumping?

KENJI: What do you think?

TIM: Maybe. What do we need to bring?

KENJI: What do we need? Well, a couple of bottles of water, some backpacks . . .

TIM: What are you thinking of having for food?

KENJI: Oh, fried egg sandwiches, chocolate cake, soda . . . What are you doing?

TIM: I'm writing it down.

KENJI: *Whaddaya *doin' this weekend?

TIM: Not much. *Whaddaya have in mind?

KENJI: Bungee jumping.

TIM: Bungee jumping?

KENJI: *Whaddaya think?

TIM: Maybe. *Whadda we need to bring?

KENJI: *Whadda we need? Well, a couple *a bottles *a water, some backpacks . . .

TIM: *Whaddaya *thinkin' *a *havin' *fer food?

KENJI: Oh, fried egg sandwiches, chocolate cake, soda . . . *Whaddaya *doin'?

TIM: I'm *writin' it down.

Listen to the entire conversation again, spoken with relaxed (fast) pronunciation.

COMPREHENSION

Answer these questions about the conversation.

1. What does Kenji want to do?
2. Does Tim want to do this? Explain.
3. Do you think Tim has ever gone bungee jumping? Explain.
4. What food does Kenji suggest?
5. Do you think this food is a good choice for bungee jumping? Explain.

Now, work with a partner and compare your answers.

PRACTICE

Close your book. You'll hear each part of the conversation spoken with relaxed pronunciation. Repeat each part using careful pronunciation.

Part 2 EXPANSION

COMPREHENSION

Listen to the conversation. The speakers use relaxed pronunciation.
Answer the questions.

1. What's Kenji's advice about food and drink before the jump?
2. Why do you think Kenji gives this advice?
3. Who wants to jump first? Explain.
4. Why do you think Tim's writing a "will"?

Work with a partner. Compare your answers. Listen again if necessary.

PRACTICE

Listen again. The conversation is spoken with relaxed pronunciation. Complete the sentences with the words you would hear if they were spoken with careful pronunciation. Then, listen once more and check your answers.

KENJI: So, _____ _____ _____ think we
      1   2   3

should do first?

TIM: _____ _____ _____ say to
    4   5   6

_____ some lunch? Should we eat before we bungee jump?
   7

KENJI: No, that's not a good idea. Tim, _____ _____
                 8   9

_____ _____ ?
  10   11

TIM: Soda.

KENJI: Water is better.

TIM: I drank all _____ my water. Could I have some _____
        12   13

_____ ?
  14

KENJI: Sure, but don't drink too much before _____ jump. Now, let's get ready.
                        15

TIM: _____ _____ we need to do?
    16   17

KENJI: Decide who's _____ first. *You* look ready.
          18

TIM: _____ _____ _____ mean? *I'm* not ready.
   19   20   21

KENJI: Tim, _____ _____ _____
       22   23   24

_____ ?
  25

TIM: My "will."

DISCUSSION

Work in small groups.

What's the most exciting outdoor activity you like or would like to do? Explain.

8 I Want to Have a Hamburger

want to ⟶ *wanna

Part 1 INTRODUCTION

CONVERSATION

Listen to each part of the conversation: first spoken with careful (slow) pronunciation; then spoken with relaxed (fast) pronunciation.

Careful (Slow) Pronunciation	Relaxed (Fast) Pronunciation
JACK: What do you want to do?	JACK: *Whaddaya *wanna do?
KAREN: I'm starving. I want to eat out.	KAREN: I'm *starvin'. I *wanna eat out.
JACK: Okay. Where do you want to eat?	JACK: Okay. Where do *ya *wanna eat?
KAREN: I'm not sure. I don't want to spend a lot of money.	KAREN: I'm not sure. I don't *wanna spend a lot *a money.
JACK: Hmm. Do you want to try Tom's Burgers?	JACK: Hmm. Do *ya *wanna try Tom's Burgers?
KAREN: Maybe. Do they have low-fat lunches?	KAREN: Maybe. Do they have low-fat lunches?
JACK: Sure. What do you want to have?	JACK: Sure. *Whaddaya *wanna have?
KAREN: I want to see the menu first.	KAREN: I *wanna see the menu first.
JACK: When do you want to go there?	JACK: When do *ya *wanna go there?
KAREN: I'm really hungry. I want to go there right now.	KAREN: I'm really hungry. I *wanna go there right now.

Listen to the entire conversation again, spoken with relaxed (fast) pronunciation.

COMPREHENSION

Answer these questions about the conversation.

1. In choosing a restaurant, what's important to Karen?
2. What kind of place is Tom's?

3. What kinds of food do you think you would find there?
4. How much do you think this food would cost?
5. Has either Karen or Jack been to Tom's before? Explain.

Now, work with a partner and compare your answers.

PRACTICE

Close your book. You'll hear each part of the conversation spoken with relaxed pronunciation. Repeat each part using careful pronunciation.

Part 2 EXPANSION

COMPREHENSION

Listen to the conversation. The speakers use relaxed pronunciation.
Answer the questions.

1. What do Jack and Karen order for lunch?
2. Whose lunch is better? Why?
3. What doesn't Karen want to have? What could be the reason?
4. Who should pay for the lunches?
5. What's another way to offer to pay for someone's lunch?
6. Choose a more nutritious lunch for Jack and Karen. Explain your choices.
7. What would you order if you were eating at Tom's Burgers?

Work with a partner. Compare your answers. Listen again if necessary.

PRACTICE

Listen again. The conversation is spoken with relaxed pronunciation. Complete the sentences with the words you would hear if they were spoken with careful pronunciation. Then, listen once more and check your answers.

JACK: _____ _____ _____ _____
            1   2   3   4
_____ have?
        5

KAREN: Let's see. I _____ _____ try a chicken sandwich.
                         6   7

JACK: I _____ _____ have a cheeseburger and some fries.
            8   9

_____ _____ _____ _____
        10   11   12   13
_____ drink?
        14

KAREN: I don't _____ _____ have a lot _____
                      15   16   17
sugar. I'll have a large apple juice.

JACK: I _____ _____ try a chocolate shake. I hear the
            18   19
shakes here are very good.

CLERK: Can I help _____ ?
                          20

KAREN: We _____ _____ order a chicken sandwich, a
                  21   22
cheeseburger, one order _____ fries, a large apple juice, and a
                                23
chocolate shake.

CLERK: That'll be $11.15.

JACK: Here _____ are.
                  24

KAREN: (*to Jack*) No, no. I _____ _____ pay
                                    25   26
_____ _____ lunch. *You* paid _____
        27   28   29
my lunch last time.

JACK: But—

KAREN: No. I insist.

JACK: Thank you. That's really nice _____ _____ .
                                            30   31

KAREN: (*to the clerk*) Here _____ are. (*She hands the clerk a $20 bill.*)
32

CLERK: (*counting back the change*) $11.20, $.25, $.50, $.75, $12.00, $13.00, $14.00, $15.00 and $20.00.

Thank _____ very much.
33

KAREN: Thank *you*.

DISCUSSION

Work in small groups.

Make a list of everything you ate yesterday. How nutritious was this food? Discuss.

9 We're Going to See "The Monster That Ate Cleveland"

going to + verb ⟶ *gonna

The *gonna pronunciation isn't used when there's
no verb following *to.* EXAMPLE:
    I'm *going to* a movie.

Part 1 INTRODUCTION

CONVERSATION

Listen to each part of the conversation: first spoken with careful (slow) pronunciation;
then spoken with relaxed (fast) pronunciation.

Careful (Slow) Pronunciation	Relaxed (Fast) Pronunciation
LISA: Oh, are you going to pay our bills tonight?	LISA: Oh, are *ya *gonna pay our bills tonight?
ANN: I'm going to try.	ANN: I'm *gonna try.
LISA: Thanks. I want to handle our money soon, but I'm so busy. So, what are you going to pay first?	LISA: Thanks. I *wanna handle our money soon, but I'm so busy. So, *whaddaya *gonna pay first?
ANN: First? Well, we're not going to have enough money for this month's electric bill.	ANN: First? Well, we're not *gonna have enough money *fer this month's electric bill.
LISA: You're not going to pay this month's electric bill?	LISA: *Yer not *gonna pay this month's electric bill?
ANN: Oh, I'm going to pay it, but not right now.	ANN: Oh, I'm *gonna pay it, but not right now.
LISA: When are you going to pay it?	LISA: When are *ya *gonna pay it?
ANN: I'm going to pay it after I pay last month's water bill.	ANN: I'm *gonna pay it after I pay last month's water bill.
LISA: You haven't paid last month's water bill?	LISA: *Ya haven't paid last month's water bill?
ANN: No. I'm going to pay last month's rent first.	ANN: No. I'm *gonna pay last month's rent first.

Listen to the entire conversation again, spoken with relaxed (fast) pronunciation.

COMPREHENSION

Answer these questions about the conversation.

1. What do you think the relationship between Lisa and Ann is?
2. Why doesn't Lisa pay their bills?
3. Does Ann do a good job with their money? Explain.
4. Should Lisa let Ann pay their bills? Explain.
5. Did Lisa know about the problems with their bills? Explain.
6. What do you think Lisa will say next?

Now, work with a partner and compare your answers.

PRACTICE

Close your book. You'll hear each part of the conversation spoken with relaxed pronunciation. Repeat each part using careful pronunciation.

Part 2 EXPANSION

COMPREHENSION

Listen to the conversation. The speakers use relaxed pronunciation. Answer the questions.

1. How old do you think Linda and Lisa are? Why?
2. Is Lisa sad? Explain.
3. What kind of movie are Linda and her sister going to see?
4. Why do you think Lisa asks if it's a comedy?
5. Why does Lisa want Ann to come to the movie?

Work with a partner. Compare your answers. Listen again if necessary.

PRACTICE

Listen again. The conversation is spoken with relaxed pronunciation. Complete the sentences with the words you would hear if they were spoken with careful pronunciation. Then, listen once more and check your answers.

LINDA: So Lisa, _____(1) _____(2) _____(3) _____(4) _____(5) do tonight?

LISA: Nothing. I'm just _____(6) _____(7) stay home.

LINDA: _____(8) sound like _____(9) depressed. What's wrong?

LISA: Oh, I just have a couple _____(10) problems with my roommate. It's nothing. Are *you* _____(11) _____(12) do anything tonight?

LINDA: My sister and I are _____(13) to a movie. Do _____(14) _____(15) _____(16) come with us?

LISA: Well, maybe I should. _____(17) _____(18) _____(19) _____(20) _____(21) see?

LINDA: *The Monster That Ate Cleveland.*

LISA: Is that a comedy?

LINDA: No. It's a horror movie.

LISA: The monster ate all _____(22) Cleveland? Wow! I don't _____(23) _____(24) miss that. How soon are _____(25) _____(26) _____(27) _____(28) _____(29) leave?

LINDA: We're _____(30) _____(31) _____(32) _____(33) leave in about fifteen minutes. Does _____(34) roommate _____(35) _____(36) come with us?

LISA: Ann? That's a good idea. Maybe we'll be able to talk about our problems after the movie.

DISCUSSION

Work in small groups.

What's your favorite movie? Why?

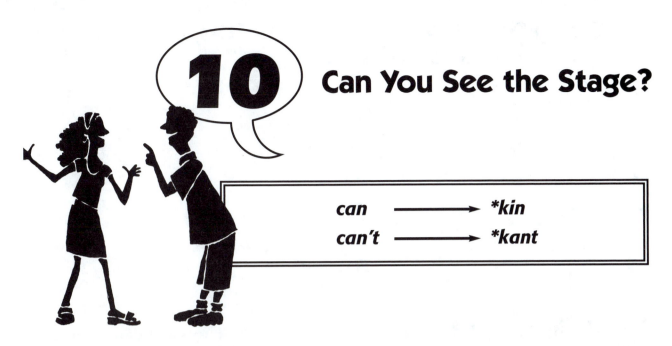

10 Can You See the Stage?

can   ⟶   *kin

can't   ⟶   *kant

Part 1 INTRODUCTION

CONVERSATION

Listen to each part of the conversation: first spoken with careful (slow) pronunciation; then spoken with relaxed (fast) pronunciation.

Careful (Slow) Pronunciation	Relaxed (Fast) Pronunciation
CARLOS: I'm going to take a singing class. Do you want to take it with me?	CARLOS: I'm *gonna take a singing class. Do *ya *wanna take it with me?
TINA: I don't need a class. I can sing. My mother says I sound great.	TINA: I don't need a class. I *kin sing. My mother says I sound great.
CARLOS: Really? I want to hear you.	CARLOS: Really? I *wanna hear *ya.
TINA: I can't sing *now.*	TINA: I *kant sing *now.*
CARLOS: Can't you just sing a few notes?	CARLOS: *Kant *ya just sing a few notes?
TINA: All right. *I'm going to love you for the rest of my life. You're my beautiful stranger.*	TINA: All right. *I'm *gonna love *ya *fer the rest *a my life. *Yer my beautiful stranger.*
CARLOS: You can't sing.	CARLOS: *Ya *kant sing.
TINA: What do you mean I can't sing? I sing with the car radio every day. I can sing.	TINA: *Whaddaya mean I *kant sing? I sing with the car radio every day. I *kin sing.
CARLOS: I'm sorry. You're right. You sound really great. Can you write songs, too?	CARLOS: I'm sorry. *Yer right. *Ya sound really great. *Kin *ya write songs, too?
TINA: No. I can sing, but I can't write songs.	TINA: No. I *kin sing, but I *kant write songs.

Listen to the entire conversation again, spoken with relaxed (fast) pronunciation.

COMPREHENSION

Answer these questions about the conversation.

1. Can Tina sing? Explain.
2. Why do you think Tina insists she can sing?
3. Why do you think Carlos says that she can't sing?
4. Why does Carlos apologize to Tina?
5. What are other ways for Carlos to apologize?

Now, work with a partner and compare your answers.

PRACTICE

Close your book. You'll hear each part of the conversation spoken with relaxed pronunciation. Repeat each part using careful pronunciation.

Part 2 EXPANSION

COMPREHENSION

Listen to the conversation. The speakers use relaxed pronunciation.
Answer the questions.

1. What do you think the relationship between Carlos and Tina is? Explain.
2. Where are they?
3. Why can't they hear each other?
4. What kind of music do you think they're listening to? Explain.
5. What does Tina need Carlos to do with her popcorn? Why?
6. What does Carlos think she needs? Why?

Work with a partner. Compare your answers. Listen again if necessary.

PRACTICE

Listen again. The conversation is spoken with relaxed pronunciation. Complete the sentences with the words you would hear if they were spoken with careful pronunciation. Then, listen once more and check your answers.

CARLOS: _____ _____ see the stage, Tina?
              1   2

TINA: No. I _____ see over the head _____ the man in
              3   4

  front _____ me. _____ _____ change
            5   6   7

  seats with me?

CARLOS: Sure. _____ _____ see better now?
               8   9

TINA: Yes. Thanks. Look! The band's _____ _____ start
                          10   11

  _____ .
     12

CARLOS: Aren't they great? Do _____ like the music?
                          13

TINA: _____ _____ _____ _____ ?
      14   15   16   17

  I _____ hear _____ . _____
       18   19   20

  _____ speak up?
     21

CARLOS: Are _____ _____ the music?
             22   23

TINA: _____ _____ speak up? The Raging Onions
      24   25

  are _____ so loudly, we _____ hear each other!
       26   27

CARLOS: Do _____ like the music? I _____ talk any
             28   29

  louder!

TINA: I love the music! I _____ _____ take a picture, but I
                      30   31

  _____ hold the popcorn at the same time. _____
     32   33

  _____ hold my popcorn _____ a minute?
     34   35

CARLOS: Sure. I _____ get _____ more popcorn.
             36   37

DISCUSSION

Work in small groups.

Who's your favorite singer? Why?

11 What Can I Get You for Your Cold?

get ———————➔ *git

Part 1 INTRODUCTION

CONVERSATION

Listen to each part of the conversation: first spoken with careful (slow) pronunciation; then spoken with relaxed (fast) pronunciation.

Careful (Slow) Pronunciation

JEAN: Can I get you some chicken soup, honey?

NICK: No, I don't want to eat anything. My stomach's really hurting.

JEAN: Okay, but I'm going to get you some juice. You need liquids for your cough.

NICK: Can you get me some apple juice?

JEAN: Okay.

NICK: Oh, get me a straw, too.

JEAN: Sure.

NICK: Can I get up now, Mom?

JEAN: You can't get up until your fever goes away, honey.

NICK: Then, Mom, can you get me something to do? I'm *really* bored.

Relaxed (Fast) Pronunciation

JEAN: *Kin I *git *ya some chicken soup, honey?

NICK: No, I don't *wanna eat anything. My stomach's really *hurtin'.

JEAN: Okay, but I'm *gonna *git *ya some juice. *Ya need liquids *fer *yer cough.

NICK: *Kin *ya *git me some apple juice?

JEAN: Okay.

NICK: Oh, *git me a straw, too.

JEAN: Sure.

NICK: *Kin I *git up now, Mom?

JEAN: *Ya *kant *git up until *yer fever goes away, honey.

NICK: Then, Mom, *kin *ya *git me something to do? I'm *really* bored.

Listen to the entire conversation again, spoken with relaxed (fast) pronunciation.

COMPREHENSION

Answer these questions about the conversation.

1. What's the relationship between Jean and Nick?
2. How old do you think Nick is? Explain.
3. Who can you call "honey"?
4. What are Nick's symptoms?
5. Why do you think Nick is bored?

Now, work with a partner and compare your answers.

PRACTICE

Close your book. You'll hear each part of the conversation spoken with relaxed pronunciation. Repeat each part using careful pronunciation.

Part 2 EXPANSION

COMPREHENSION

Listen to the conversation. The speakers use relaxed pronunciation. Answer the questions.

1. What's the relationship between Jean and Andrea?
2. Do you think it's a good relationship? Explain.
3. Who is sick?
4. What medicines does Jean need?
5. What's each medicine for?
6. Why do you think Jean needs sleep?

Work with a partner. Compare your answers. Listen again if necessary.

PRACTICE

Listen again. The conversation is spoken with relaxed pronunciation. Complete the sentences with the words you would hear if they were spoken with careful pronunciation. Then, listen once more and check your answers.

ANDREA: Hi, Jean.

JEAN: Hi, Andrea. Come in.

ANDREA: How are _____ 1 _____ 2 ?

JEAN: I'm fine, but Nick's still sick.

ANDREA: Oh? That's too bad. Kids _____ 3 sick a lot. _____ 4 I _____ 5 _____ 6 anything at the pharmacy? I'm _____ 7 _____ 8 go there, anyway.

JEAN: *You* are? Thanks so much. _____ 9 a great sister.

ANDREA: No problem. You'd do the same _____ 10 me. So, _____ 11 _____ 12 _____ 13 need?

JEAN: _____ 14 _____ 15 _____ 16 some children's cough syrup? Oh! And _____ 17 _____ 18 _____ 19 me some antacid _____ 20 Nick's stomach?

ANDREA: I'd better _____ 21 some Tylenol, too. I borrowed _____ 22 _____ 23 my kids last week, remember? It's at my house.

JEAN: Oh, okay. Great. I guess that's it.

ANDREA: Not quite. What _____ 24 I _____ 25 _____ 26 _____ 27 *your* cough?

JEAN: What cough?

ANDREA: That cough. What _____ 28 I _____ 29 _____ 30 ?

JEAN: _____ 31 _____ 32 _____ 33 me some sleep?

That's what I really need!

DISCUSSION

Work in small groups.

What do you do for a cold? What medicines do you take? What foods do you eat?

12 Take Bus 4 to Second Street

to ——→ *ta

To isn't pronounced *ta* if it's stressed or if it's not followed by another word. EXAMPLE: **Who do I give it *to*?**

Part 1 INTRODUCTION

CONVERSATION

Listen to each part of the conversation: first spoken with careful (slow) pronunciation; then spoken with relaxed (fast) pronunciation.

Careful (Slow) Pronunciation	Relaxed (Fast) Pronunciation
KATHY: Excuse me. I'm going to the mall. What bus do I take?	KATHY: Excuse me. I'm *goin' *ta the mall. What bus do I take?
MAN: Take Bus 4 to Second Street. Then you need to transfer to another bus.	MAN: Take Bus 4 *ta Second Street. Then *ya need *ta transfer *ta another bus.
KATHY: What bus do I need to transfer to?	KATHY: What bus do I need *ta transfer to?
MAN: You want to take Bus 89. It goes straight to the mall.	MAN: *Ya *wanna take Bus 89. It goes straight *ta the mall.
KATHY: Do I need to have exact change?	KATHY: Do I need *ta have exact change?
MAN: Yes. You need to put the exact change in the fare box on Bus 4.	MAN: Yes. *Ya need *ta put the exact change in the fare box on Bus 4.
KATHY: Do I need to pay again on Bus 89?	KATHY: Do I need *ta pay again on Bus 89?
MAN: No. Ask the driver of Bus 4 to give you a transfer to Bus 89.	MAN: No. Ask the driver *a Bus 4 *ta give *ya a transfer *ta Bus 89.
KATHY: What do you do with the transfer? Do you put it in the fare box?	KATHY: *Whaddaya do with the transfer? Do *ya put it in the fare box?
MAN: No. You give it to the driver of Bus 89.	MAN: No. *Ya give it *ta the driver *a Bus 89.

Listen to the entire conversation again, spoken with relaxed (fast) pronunciation.

COMPREHENSION

Answer these questions about the conversation.

1. Where's Kathy going?
2. Do you think she often goes there by bus? Explain.
3. Which buses does she have to take to get there?
4. What does she need to do with the exact change for the fare?
5. How many times does she have to pay the fare? Explain.

Now, work with a partner and compare your answers.

PRACTICE

Close your book. You'll hear each part of the conversation spoken with relaxed pronunciation. Repeat each part using careful pronunciation.

Part 2 EXPANSION

COMPREHENSION

Listen to the conversation. The speakers use relaxed pronunciation. Answer the questions.

1. Why does Kathy say, "Excuse me"?
2. What do you think are other situations where you use "excuse me"?
3. What does Kathy need?
4. What's her "problem"?
5. How does the woman respond to Kathy's problem?

Work with a partner. Compare your answers. Listen again if necessary.

PRACTICE

Listen again. The conversation is spoken with relaxed pronunciation. Complete the sentences with the words you would hear if they were spoken with careful pronunciation. Then, listen once more and check your answers.

KATHY: Excuse me. Is this Bus 89?

WOMAN AT THE BUS STOP: Yes. Where do _____ need _____ go?
                                                    1   2

KATHY: _____ the mall. Is it far?
              3

WOMAN: The Nature Mall?

KATHY: Yes.

WOMAN: I work part time at the mall. It's not far. I'll tell _____
                                                                              4

when _____ _____ off.
            5   6

KATHY: Thanks. That's really nice. _____ _____ answer a
                                              7   8

question _____ me?
                9

WOMAN: Sure. _____ _____ _____
                      10   11   12

_____ _____ know?
        13   14

KATHY: _____ _____ _____ think
              15   16   17

is the best place _____ shop at the mall?
                          18

WOMAN: Well, it depends. _____ _____ _____
                                  19   20   21

_____ _____ _____ _____ buy?
        22   23   24   25

KATHY: I need _____ _____ some shoes. But my feet are a little
                    26   27

big. I need _____ find one _____ those large-size shoe stores.
                  28   29

WOMAN: _____ feet don't look big. They look fine.
              30

KATHY: Thanks. That's nice _____ hear. I need _____ find some
                                  31   32

casual shoes. I also need _____ _____ some dress shoes.
                                  33   34

WOMAN: Well, there are plenty _____ places _____ shop. I'm
                                      35   36

sure you'll be able _____ find some nice shoes.
                            37

DISCUSSION

Work in small groups.

What's the best kind of transportation you've ever used? Why?

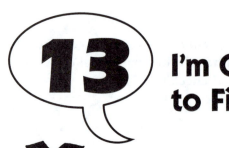

13 I'm Going to Try to Find a Job

---

to after a vowel sound ⟶ *da

The reduced form *da* is common after *go. To* isn't pronounced *da* if stressed or if it's not followed by another word. EXAMPLE:
    A: *Kin *ya fix this?
    B: There's no way *to.*

Part 1 INTRODUCTION

CONVERSATION

Listen to each part of the conversation: first spoken with careful (slow) pronunciation; then spoken with relaxed (fast) pronunciation.

Careful (Slow) Pronunciation	Relaxed (Fast) Pronunciation
BILL: I want to go to Spain.	BILL: I *wanna go *da Spain.
DAD: You want to go to Spain?	DAD: *Ya *wanna go *da Spain?
BILL: Yes.	BILL: Yes.
DAD: Why do you want to go to Spain?	DAD: Why do *ya *wanna go *da Spain?
BILL: I want to try to learn about other cultures.	BILL: I *wanna try *da learn about other cultures.
DAD: That's a really good idea, but who's going to pay for your trip?	DAD: That's a really good idea, but who's *gonna pay *fer *yer trip?
BILL: Well, *you* are.	BILL: Well, *you* are.
DAD: You want *me* to pay for it?	DAD: *Ya want *me* *da pay *fer it?
BILL: Well, I already tried to get the money from Mom.	BILL: Well, I already tried *ta *git the money from Mom.
DAD: I know a better way to get the money. Try to find a job.	DAD: I know a better way *da *git the money. Try *da find a job.

Listen to the entire conversation again, spoken with relaxed (fast) pronunciation.

COMPREHENSION

Answer these questions about the conversation.

1. What does Bill want to do? Why?
2. How old do you think he is? Explain.
3. What's Bill's problem?
4. How does he try to solve his problem?
5. What's his father's solution to the problem?
6. Do you think this is a good solution? Explain.

Now, work with a partner and compare your answers.

PRACTICE

Close your book. You'll hear each part of the conversation spoken with relaxed pronunciation. Repeat each part using careful pronunciation.

Part 2 EXPANSION

COMPREHENSION

Listen to the conversation. The speakers use relaxed pronunciation. Answer the questions.

1. Where do you think Bill and Mohammed are? Explain.
2. What does Bill want? Why?
3. What do you think are other ways to find what Bill wants?
4. How does Bill look for a job on the Internet?
5. Is a dog trainer a job in the movie industry? Explain.
6. Do you think Bill wants this job? Explain.

Work with a partner. Compare your answers. Listen again if necessary.

PRACTICE

Listen again. The conversation is spoken with relaxed pronunciation. Complete the sentences with the words you would hear if they were spoken with careful pronunciation. Then, listen once more and check your answers.

BILL: Mohammed, I'm _____ 1 _____ 2 _____ 3
_____ 4 the market _____ 5 _____ 6 a newspaper.
I need _____ 7 try _____ 8 find a job.

MOHAMMED: Why, Bill?

BILL: Because I _____ 9 _____ 10 _____ 11
_____ 12 Spain. It costs a lot _____ 13 money _____ 14
go there.

MOHAMMED: So, ask _____ 15 dad.

BILL: I did. He wants *me* _____ 16 pay _____ 17 the trip.

MOHAMMED: Oh. Well, do _____ 18 _____ 19 _____ 20
try _____ 21 find a job on the Internet?

BILL: I don't know how _____ 22 do that. _____ 23
_____ 24 help me?

MOHAMMED: Sure. It's easy. First, go _____ 25 the Internet. Type the word "job."
Then choose the kind _____ 26 jobs _____ 27 _____ 28
_____ 29 try _____ 30 find — education, health care, business . . .

BILL: Could I try _____ 31 find something in the movie industry?

MOHAMMED: Sure.

BILL: Okay. I did it.

MOHAMMED: Now choose the city _____ 32 _____ 33
_____ 34 work in. See? It's really easy _____ 35 do.
There's the first one!

BILL: Dog trainer? Maybe I should look _____ 36 something in sales.

DISCUSSION

Work in small groups. When is someone old enough to get a job? Explain.

14 I've Got to Check Your Teeth

got to	⟶	*gotta
have to	⟶	*hafta
has to	⟶	*hasta

Part 1 INTRODUCTION

CONVERSATION

Listen to each part of the conversation: first spoken with careful (slow) pronunciation; then spoken with relaxed (fast) pronunciation.

Careful (Slow) Pronunciation	Relaxed (Fast) Pronunciation
JOE: My tooth's driving me crazy.	JOE: My tooth's *drivin' me crazy.
GEORGE: Then you've got to make an appointment with a dentist.	GEORGE: Then you've *gotta make an appointment with a dentist.
JOE: I've got to find one first. I don't have a dentist.	JOE: I've *gotta find one first. I don't have a dentist.
GEORGE: I have to go downtown. Come on. Let's go to *my* dentist.	GEORGE: I *hafta go downtown. Come on. Let's go *da *my* dentist.
JOE: I can't. I have to study.	JOE: I *kant. I *hafta study.
GEORGE: Are you going to go to the dentist after that? Your tooth has to be taken care of.	GEORGE: Are *ya *gonna go *da the dentist after that? *Yer tooth *hasta be taken care of.
JOE: I know it has to be taken care of. But I've got to get some gas.	JOE: I know it *hasta be taken care of. But I've *gotta *git some gas.
GEORGE: *Then* are you going to go to the dentist?	GEORGE: *Then* are *ya *gonna go *da the dentist?
JOE: Well, no. After that, I have to go to the bank.	JOE: Well, no. After that, I *hafta go *da the bank.
GEORGE: Okay, but after you go to the bank, you've got to go to the dentist!	GEORGE: Okay, but after *ya go *da the bank, you've *gotta go *da the dentist!

Listen to the entire conversation again, spoken with relaxed (fast) pronunciation.

COMPREHENSION

Answer these questions about the conversation.

1. What's Joe's problem?
2. Why can't Joe make an appointment with a dentist?
3. Do you think Joe is really too busy to see the dentist? Explain.
4. Do you think Joe visits the dentist often? Explain.

Now, work with a partner and compare your answers.

PRACTICE

Close your book. You'll hear each part of the conversation spoken with relaxed pronunciation. Repeat each part using careful pronunciation.

Part 2 EXPANSION

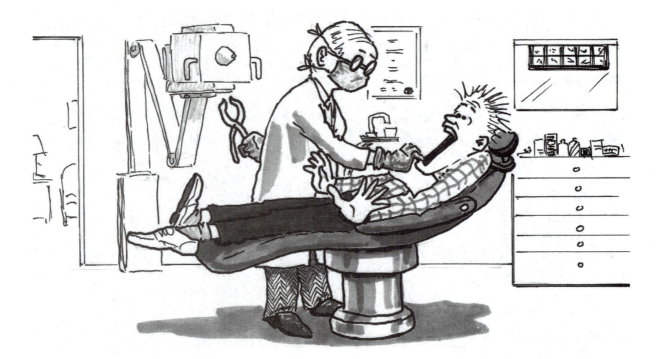

COMPREHENSION

Listen to the conversation. The speakers use relaxed pronunciation. Answer the questions.

1. What's Joe worried about?
2. What did the dentist do?
3. What's the dentist going to do tomorrow?
4. How often do you think Joe should see the dentist? Why?

Work with a partner. Compare your answers. Listen again if necessary.

PRACTICE

Listen again. The conversation is spoken with relaxed pronunciation. Complete the sentences with the words you would hear if they were spoken with careful pronunciation. Then, listen once more and check your answers.

JOE: The dentist has _____(1)_____ _____(2)_____ see me soon. My tooth really hurts! He _____(3)_____ _____(4)_____ do something about it.

GEORGE: Don't worry, Joe. I'm sure the dentist is _____(5)_____ _____(6)_____ be able _____(7)_____ help _____(8)_____ . _____(9)_____ won't _____(10)_____ _____(11)_____ wait very long.

JOE: _____(12)_____ don't think the dentist is _____(13)_____ _____(14)_____ tell me he _____(15)_____ _____(16)_____ pull my tooth, do _____(17)_____ ?

GEORGE: I'm not sure. If the dentist _____(18)_____ _____(19)_____ pull it, he will, but I'm sure he'll try _____(20)_____ save it if he _____(21)_____ .

JOE: Well, I guess I won't _____(22)_____ _____(23)_____ wait any longer _____(24)_____ find out. He's ready _____(25)_____ see me now.

(Later)

GEORGE: What happened?

JOE: Well, first he said he'd _____(26)_____ _____(27)_____ check the tooth.

GEORGE: Then what happened? Did he _____(28)_____ _____(29)_____ pull it?

JOE: No. He decided _____(30)_____ fill it, not pull it. But he said I've _____(31)_____ _____(32)_____ come back tomorrow. He's _____(33)_____ _____(34)_____ take some x-rays, and he _____(35)_____ _____(36)_____ check my other teeth.

GEORGE: You've _____(37)_____ _____(38)_____ see the dentist more often!

DISCUSSION

Work in small groups.

Do your family and friends go to the dentist regularly? How often do you go to the dentist? How often should you go? Discuss.

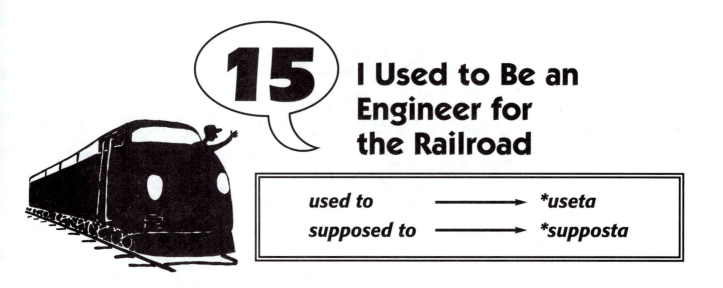

15 I Used to Be an Engineer for the Railroad

used to	⟶	***useta***
supposed to	⟶	***supposta***

Part 1 INTRODUCTION

CONVERSATION

Listen to each part of the conversation: first spoken with careful (slow) pronunciation; then spoken with relaxed (fast) pronunciation.

Careful (Slow) Pronunciation	Relaxed (Fast) Pronunciation
HENRY: Is my breakfast ready yet? I want to go to the park.	HENRY: Is my breakfast ready yet? I *wanna go *da the park.
OLGA: Not yet. You know, before he died, my first husband used to cook breakfast for me every Sunday.	OLGA: Not yet. *Ya know, before he died, my first husband *useta cook breakfast *fer me every Sunday.
HENRY: Manuel used to cook for *you*? Men aren't supposed to cook.	HENRY: Manuel *useta cook *fer *you*? Men aren't *supposta cook.
OLGA: What do you mean, men aren't supposed to cook?	OLGA: *Whaddaya mean, men aren't *supposta cook?
HENRY: Women are supposed to cook.	HENRY: Women are *supposta cook.
OLGA: He used to sew curtains for us, too.	OLGA: He *useta sew curtains *fer us, too.
HENRY: You're kidding, right? Men aren't supposed to sew. Before my first wife died, she used to always say—	HENRY: *Yer *kiddin', right? Men aren't *supposta sew. Before my first wife died, she *useta always say—
OLGA: Nina used to ride a Harley-Davidson motorcycle to work, didn't she?	OLGA: Nina *useta ride a Harley-Davidson motorcycle *ta work, didn't she?
HENRY: Well, yes, but she used to ride it *after* she made my breakfast.	HENRY: Well, yes, but she *useta ride it *after* she made my breakfast.

Listen to the entire conversation again, spoken with relaxed (fast) pronunciation.

COMPREHENSION

Answer these questions about the conversation.

1. What do you think the relationship between Henry and Olga is?
2. What does Henry think a woman should do?
3. What does Olga think a man should do?
4. Have Henry and Olga been married before? Explain.
5. What do you know about Olga's first husband?
6. What do you know about Henry's first wife?

Now, work with a partner and compare your answers.

PRACTICE

Close your book. You'll hear each part of the conversation spoken with relaxed pronunciation. Repeat each part using careful pronunciation.

Part 2 EXPANSION

COMPREHENSION

Listen to the conversation. The speakers use relaxed pronunciation. Answer the questions.

1. Where do you think Henry and Jack are?
2. How old do you think they are? Explain.
3. In what ways is the world changing too fast for them?
4. Do you think they know each other well? Why or why not?
5. What do you know about Henry?
6. What do you know about Jack?

Work with a partner. Compare your answers. Listen again if necessary.

PRACTICE

Listen again. The conversation is spoken with relaxed pronunciation. Complete the sentences with the words you would hear if they were spoken with careful pronunciation. Then, listen once more and check your answers.

HENRY: _____ _____ ask _____ a better day
            1   2   3

than today.

JACK: No. _____ _____ .
             4   5

HENRY: I was _____ _____ stay home and cook breakfast
               6   7

this morning. My wife doesn't _____ _____ cook
                             8   9

breakfast on Sundays. But it's too nice a day _____ stay home.
                                         10

JACK: _____ right. It's a beautiful day. _____ not
           11   12

_____ _____ stay inside on a day like today.
        13   14

HENRY: I completely agree. _____ know, I _____
                       15   16

_____ go _____ the park on Seventh Avenue.
    17   18

Do _____ remember that park? They tore it down _____
          19   20

build a shopping mall.

JACK: Yeah. That was terrible. I _____ _____ go there after work.
                          21   22

HENRY: Aren't we _____ _____ care more about parks than
                    23   24

buildings?

Jack: We're _____ _____ . Yeah. The world's _____
             25   26   27

too fast _____ me.
          28

HENRY: Me, too. By the way, my name's Henry.

JACK: Nice _____ meet _____ , Henry. My name's Jack.
          29   30

HENRY: So, Jack, what kind _____ work did _____ do?
                     31   32

JACK: I _____ _____ be a farmer. I raised wheat.
         33   34

HENRY: Oh? I _____ _____ be an engineer _____
          35   36   37

the railroad. I was an engineer _____ fifty years.
                           38

JACK: I _____ _____ be married _____ a
        39   40   41

wonderful woman.

HENRY: Was she a good cook?

JACK: Oh, yeah. She _____ _____ cook wonderful meals.
                          42   43

HENRY: Wives are _____ _____ cook _____
                          44   45   46
    their husbands, aren't they?

JACK: Oh, yeah. Definitely. They're _____ _____ cook,
                                              47   48
    clean, sew, all _____ that stuff.
                          49

HENRY: That's not an old-fashioned idea, is it?

JACK: Not _____ me.
                    50

DISCUSSION

Work in small groups.

Should a man cook, sew, or clean the house? Should a woman make money, fix a car, or ride a motorcycle? Explain.

16 What's the Fastest Way to Send His Packages?

he	→ *'e
his	→ *'is
him	→ *'im
her	→ *'er
them	→ *'em

These pronunciations are not used when *he, his, him, her,* and *them* are stressed.

Part 1 INTRODUCTION

CONVERSATION

Listen to each part of the conversation: first spoken with careful (slow) pronunciation; then spoken with relaxed (fast) pronunciation.

Careful (Slow) Pronunciation	Relaxed (Fast) Pronunciation
MICHIKO: Can you help me?	MICHIKO: *Kin *ya help me?
PAULA: Sure. What do you need?	PAULA: Sure. *Whaddaya need?
MICHIKO: Well, I'm going to mail these packages to my parents. I want them to get them as soon as possible.	MICHIKO: Well, I'm *gonna mail these packages *ta my parents. I want *'em *ta *git *'em as soon as possible.
PAULA: How fast do you want them to get them?	PAULA: How fast do *ya want *'em *ta *git *'em?
MICHIKO: Faster than my brother got the package I sent *him.*	MICHIKO: Faster than my brother got the package I sent *him.*
PAULA: When did he get it?	PAULA: When did *'e *git it?
MICHIKO: Well, I sent him the package last month. Do you know when he got it? Last week!	MICHIKO: Well, I sent *'im the package last month. Do *ya know when *'e got it? Last week!
PAULA: How did you send it?	PAULA: How did *ya send it?
MICHIKO: I sent his package first class.	MICHIKO: I sent *'is package first class.
PAULA: Wow. I sent my sister a package, and it only took her four days to get it.	PAULA: Wow. I sent my sister a package, and it only took *'er four days *ta *git it.

Listen to the entire conversation again, spoken with relaxed (fast) pronunciation.

COMPREHENSION

Answer these questions about the conversation.

1. What's Michiko's problem?
2. Michiko says, "I want them to get them as soon as possible." Who or what is the first "them"? Who or what is the second "them"?
3. Why could Michiko's package have taken so long to get to her brother?
4. How do you think Paula sent the package to her sister?
5. Does Paula help Michiko with her problem? Explain.

Now, work with a partner and compare your answers.

PRACTICE

Close your book. You'll hear each part of the conversation spoken with relaxed pronunciation. Repeat each part using careful pronunciation.

Part 2 EXPANSION

COMPREHENSION

Listen to the conversation. The speakers use relaxed pronunciation.
Answer the questions.

1. Where are Michiko and the clerk?
2. Why does the clerk want to talk to his supervisor?
3. What are the two best ways to send Michiko's packages?
4. Which packages have to arrive first—her parents' or her uncle's? Explain.
5. Why do you think the packages to Michiko's uncle have to arrive by Friday?

Work with a partner. Compare your answers. Listen again if necessary.

PRACTICE

Listen again. The conversation is spoken with relaxed pronunciation. Complete the sentences with the words you would hear if they were spoken with careful pronunciation. Then, listen once more and check your answers.

MICHIKO: Hi. I _____ 1 _____ 2 send these packages
_____ 3 New York.

CLERK: How do _____ 4 _____ 5 _____ 6 send
_____ 7 ?

MICHIKO: I'm not sure. I'm _____ 8 _____ 9 _____ 10
my uncle, and I _____ 11 _____ 12 _____ 13
_____ 14 to _____ 15 by Friday. _____ 16
_____ 17 _____ 18 suggest?

CLERK: I'm new here. I'll go talk _____ 19 my supervisor. I'll ask
_____ 20 what the fastest way would be.

MICHIKO: Tell _____ 21 that they _____ 22 _____ 23
_____ 24 _____ 25 my uncle as soon as possible, and
that _____ 26 _____ 27 _____ 28 _____ 29
_____ 30 no later than Friday.

CLERK: I'll tell _____ 31 .

(A few minutes later)

MICHIKO: What's _____ 32 advice?

CLERK: She says _____ 33 should send _____ 34 to
_____ 35 by Priority Mail or Express Mail. Express Mail's the fastest, but it's
expensive. If _____ 36 send _____ 37 _____ 38
_____ 39 uncle by Priority Mail, it's cheaper, but _____ 40
might not _____ 41 _____ 42 _____ 43 a few days.

MICHIKO: If I send _____ 44 packages to _____ 45 by Priority Mail,
will _____ 46 _____ 47 _____ 48 by Friday?

CLERK: Maybe. If _____ luck's good, _____ will, but I
49   50

_____ promise anything.
51

MICHIKO: Then I'll send my uncle _____ packages by Express Mail.
52

I'm also _____ _____ send some packages _____
53   54   55

my parents. I guess I'll send my parents' packages by Priority Mail. Thanks.

CLERK: _____ welcome.
56

DISCUSSION

Work in small groups.

What's the worst experience you've ever had sending or receiving mail? Explain.

17 We Arrive on Tuesday and Leave on Thursday

and ——————————→ *'n'
And isn't pronounced *'n' if stressed.

Part 1 INTRODUCTION

CONVERSATION

Listen to each part of the conversation: first spoken with careful (slow) pronunciation; then spoken with relaxed (fast) pronunciation.

Careful (Slow) Pronunciation	Relaxed (Fast) Pronunciation
JULIE: I want to make a reservation for Tuesday, April 6.	JULIE: I *wanna make a reservation *fer Tuesday, April 6.
RESERVATIONS: We have a single room and a double room available for the sixth.	RESERVATIONS: We have a single room *'n' a double room available *fer the sixth.
JULIE: Does the double have a refrigerator and an extra bed?	JULIE: Does the double have a refrigerator *'n' an extra bed?
RESERVATIONS: It has a refrigerator, and we can get you a rollaway bed.	RESERVATIONS: It has a refrigerator, *'n' we *kin *git *ya a rollaway bed.
JULIE: Is it quiet? And is there a charge for children under three?	JULIE: Is it quiet? *'N' is there a charge *fer children under three?
RESERVATIONS: Yes, it's very quiet, and there's no charge for children.	RESERVATIONS: Yes, it's very quiet, *'n' there's no charge *fer children.
JULIE: Great. I'll take it. There'll be four people: myself, my husband, and two children.	JULIE: Great. I'll take it. There'll be four people: myself, my husband, *'n' two children.
RESERVATIONS: Fine. I'll need your name and a credit card number to hold that room.	RESERVATIONS: Fine. I'll need *yer name *'n' a credit card number *ta hold that room.

JULIE: My name is Julie Kim,
    K-I-M, and my credit card
    number is 453. . . .

RESERVATIONS: Excuse me. An
    airplane flew overhead, and I
    couldn't hear. What's your . . .

JULIE: My name is Julie Kim,
    K-I-M, *'n' my credit card
    number is 453. . . .

RESERVATIONS: Excuse me. An
    airplane flew overhead, *'n' I
    couldn't hear. What's *yer . . .

Listen to the entire conversation again, spoken with relaxed (fast) pronunciation.

COMPREHENSION

Answer these questions about the conversation.

1. What does Julie want? When?
2. How old do you think Julie's children are? Explain.
3. What do you know about the room?
4. Why will Julie have to repeat her credit card number?
5. Do you think Julie will like the room? Explain.

Now, work with a partner and compare your answers.

PRACTICE

Close your book. You'll hear each part of the conversation spoken with relaxed pronunciation. Repeat each part using careful pronunciation.

Part 2 EXPANSION

COMPREHENSION

Listen to the conversation. The speakers use relaxed pronunciation.
Answer the questions.

1. Where's Julie?
2. What's wrong with the room?
3. Why can't Julie order something from Room Service?
4. Do you think the front desk clerk is doing a good job? Explain.
5. Do you think Julie should complain to the manager about the hotel? Explain.

Work with a partner. Compare your answers. Listen again if necessary.

PRACTICE

Listen again. The conversation is spoken with relaxed pronunciation. Complete the sentences with the words you would hear if they were spoken with careful pronunciation. Then, listen once more and check your answers.

JULIE: Excuse me. It's 10 P.M., _____ the man next door is _____
                         1   2

    _____ _____ the guitar.
           3   4

FRONT DESK: He's _____ _____ _____ the guitar?
                          5   6   7

JULIE: Yes. _____ _____ hear _____ ?
               8   9   10

FRONT DESK: I'll send somebody _____ talk _____
                                  11   12

    _____ right away.
       13

JULIE: Thank you.

FRONT DESK: Excuse me. I _____ hear _____ . There's an
                          14   15

    airplane—

JULIE: Thank you! _____ _____ we have a rollaway bed?
                       16   17

    The reservations clerk said you'd have a rollaway bed _____ me,
                                              18

    _____ it's not here.
       19

FRONT DESK: I'll check . . . Okay, we have a rollaway bed reserved _____
                                                  20

    Room 27, _____ then _____ is right here. I'll send it up.
                   21   22

JULIE: _____ the refrigerator doesn't work. _____ we
          23   24

    order some sandwiches _____ sodas from Room Service?
                                 25

FRONT DESK: I'm sorry. Room Service closes at 10 P.M.

JULIE: We _____ order just one sandwich _____ a soda?
           26   27

FRONT DESK: Excuse me. Another airplane just—

JULIE: _____ we order a sandwich _____ a soda?
               28   29

FRONT DESK: I'm really sorry. There's a vending machine with chips _____
          30

candy at the end _____ the hall.
          31

JULIE: Chips _____ candy? That's it?
          32

FRONT DESK: Room Service opens at 8:00 A.M., _____ _____
          33   34

_____ order breakfast then. I'm really sorry.
     35

JULIE: All right. Oh, _____ one more question. Who _____
          36   37

I complain _____ about this hotel?
     38

DISCUSSION

Work in small groups.

Describe the best hotel or motel you've ever stayed at. Then describe the worst.

18 Do You Want a Chocolate or Lemon Birthday Cake?

or ⟶ *er
Or isn't pronounced ***er** if stressed.

Part 1 INTRODUCTION

CONVERSATION

Listen to each part of the conversation: first spoken with careful (slow) pronunciation; then spoken with relaxed (fast) pronunciation.

Careful (Slow) Pronunciation	Relaxed (Fast) Pronunciation
DAVID: So, do you want to have your birthday party at the park or a restaurant?	DAVID: So, do *ya *wanna have *yer birthday party at the park *er a restaurant?
JAMIE: Both.	JAMIE: Both.
DAVID: Honey, you can't have both. The park or a restaurant?	DAVID: Honey, *ya *kant have both. The park *er a restaurant?
JAMIE: I want to go to . . . the park.	JAMIE: I *wanna go *da . . . the park.
DAVID: Okay. Do you want a chocolate or a lemon birthday cake?	DAVID: Okay. Do *ya want a chocolate *er a lemon birthday cake?
JAMIE: Uh. . . both.	JAMIE: Uh . . . both.
DAVID: Honey, you have to make a choice—chocolate or lemon?	DAVID: Honey, *ya *hafta make a choice—chocolate *er lemon?
JAMIE: Chocolate.	JAMIE: Chocolate.
DAVID: Good. And which toy do you want to bring—the truck or the airplane?	DAVID: Good. *'N' which toy do *ya *wanna bring—the truck *er the airplane?
JAMIE: I don't want to bring the truck *or* the airplane. I want to get a new toy.	JAMIE: I don't *wanna bring the truck *or* the airplane. I *wanna *git a new toy.

Listen to the entire conversation again, spoken with relaxed (fast) pronunciation.

COMPREHENSION

Answer these questions about the conversation.

1. What do you think the relationship between David and Jamie is?
2. What's David planning?
3. What decisions does Jamie have to make?
4. How old do you think Jamie is? Explain.
5. Why do you think Jamie wants to get a new toy?

Now, work with a partner and compare your answers.

PRACTICE

Close your book. You'll hear each part of the conversation spoken with relaxed pronunciation. Repeat each part using careful pronunciation.

Part 2 EXPANSION

COMPREHENSION

Listen to the conversation. The speakers use relaxed pronunciation. Answer the questions.

1. Where do you think David, Brenda, and Jamie are?
2. What do you think their relationship to each other is?
3. What are they celebrating?
4. What are all of the things they do to celebrate?
5. What's Jamie's wish?
6. Why shouldn't Jamie tell anybody the wish?

Work with a partner. Compare your answers. Listen again if necessary.

PRACTICE

Listen again. The conversation is spoken with relaxed pronunciation. Complete the sentences with the words you would hear if they were spoken with careful pronunciation. Then, listen once more and check your answers.

DAVID: So, Jamie, do _____ _____ _____ play on
                   1   2   3
    the swings first _____ do _____ _____
                             4   5   6
    _____ eat?
         7

JAMIE: I _____ _____ eat first.
          8   9

BRENDA: Okay, honey. _____ _____ _____ want?
                    10   11   12
    A hot dog _____ a hamburger?
               13

JAMIE: Both.

DAVID: Both? Where are _____ _____ _____ put
                      14   15   16
    all _____ that food?
         17

JAMIE: It's my birthday. I've _____ _____ eat more now
                    18   19
    because I'm older.

BRENDA: I _____ argue with that. Do _____ want ketchup
          20   21
    _____ mustard on _____ hot dog?
      22   23

JAMIE: I want mustard. _____ I don't want anything on my hamburger.
                   24

BRENDA: Okay. Here _____ are.
              25

(Ten minutes later)

BRENDA: _____ _____ _____ think, Jamie?
          26   27   28
    Should we open _____ presents now _____ after we eat
                   29   30
    the cake?

JAMIE: After we eat the cake.

BRENDA: David, _____ _____ light the candles,
               31   32
    _____ do _____ want me _____ do it?
      33   34   35

DAVID: I'll do it.

BRENDA: Okay, Jamie, close _____ eyes, make a wish, _____
                      36   37
    blow out the candles.

DAVID: Wow! _____ blew _____ all out! Now
                      38   39

_____ _____ _____ wish.
     40   41   42

JAMIE: _____ mean, tomorrow I _____ have another birthday
            43   44

   party at a restaurant?

BRENDA: Honey, _____ not _____ _____ tell us
              45   46   47

_____ wish, _____ it won't happen.
   48   49

JAMIE: But, if I don't tell _____ my wish, how _____
                         50   51

_____ give it _____ me?
   52   53

DISCUSSION

Work in small groups.

What do you do to celebrate your birthday? Explain.

19 I Don't Know What Classes to Take

don't know ⟶ *donno

Part 1 INTRODUCTION

CONVERSATION

Listen to each part of the conversation: first spoken with careful (slow) pronunciation; then spoken with relaxed (fast) pronunciation.

Careful (Slow) Pronunciation	Relaxed (Fast) Pronunciation
TONY: I don't know what classes to take next semester.	TONY: I *donno what classes *ta take next semester.
LISA: Well, what are you thinking of taking?	LISA: Well, *whaddaya *thinkin' *a *takin'?
TONY: I don't know. The problem is that I'm going to be working afternoons.	TONY: I *donno. The problem is that I'm *gonna be *workin' afternoons.
LISA: Are you going to be working all semester?	LISA: Are *ya *gonna be *workin' all semester?
TONY: I don't know right now.	TONY: I *donno right now.
LISA: What do you want to do when you finish school?	LISA: *Whaddaya *wanna do when *ya finish school?
TONY: That's another problem. I don't know.	TONY: That's another problem. I *donno.
LISA: Do you want to talk with a counselor?	LISA: Do *ya *wanna talk with a counselor?
TONY: I don't know. What do you think?	TONY: I *donno. *Whaddaya think?
LISA: If you don't know what to do, you have to talk to somebody.	LISA: If *ya *donno what *ta do, *ya *hafta talk *ta somebody.

Listen to the entire conversation again, spoken with relaxed (fast) pronunciation.

COMPREHENSION

Answer these questions about the conversation.

1. What's Tony's problem?
2. What do you think the relationship between Tony and Lisa is?
3. How old do you think Tony is? Explain.
4. Why do you think Lisa asks him what he wants to do after he finishes school?
5. What do you think Tony finally decides to do? Why?

Now, work with a partner and compare your answers.

PRACTICE

Close your book. You'll hear each part of the conversation spoken with relaxed pronunciation. Repeat each part using careful pronunciation.

Part 2 EXPANSION

COMPREHENSION

Listen to the conversation. The speakers use relaxed pronunciation.
Answer the questions.

1. Why isn't Tony sure about taking engineering classes?
2. Do you think Tony has confidence in himself? Explain.
3. Do you think Tony really wants to be an engineer? Explain.
4. Do you think a lot of people have the same problem as Tony? Explain.
5. What would your advice to Tony be?

Work with a partner. Compare your answers. Listen again if necessary.

PRACTICE

Listen again. The conversation is spoken with relaxed pronunciation. Complete the sentences with the words you would hear if they were spoken with careful pronunciation. Then, listen once more and check your answers.

COUNSELOR: So, Tony, how are _____1_____ _____2_____ today?

TONY: I _____3_____ _____4_____ .

COUNSELOR: Well, what _____5_____ I help _____6_____ with?

TONY: I _____7_____ _____8_____ what classes _____9_____ take next semester.

COUNSELOR: _____10_____ a freshman, right?

TONY: Yes.

COUNSELOR: Okay, _____11_____ _____12_____ _____13_____ _____14_____ _____15_____ do after _____16_____ graduate?

TONY: I _____17_____ _____18_____ .

COUNSELOR: There's nothing _____19_____ _____20_____ _____21_____ do?

TONY: Well, my grandfather _____22_____ _____23_____ be an engineer. I'm _____24_____ about studying engineering, but I _____25_____ _____26_____ if I'll do well.

COUNSELOR: We have some excellent engineering classes _____27_____ _____28_____ take. Have _____29_____ talked _____30_____ _____31_____ parents about this, Tony?

TONY: No. They _____32_____ _____33_____ yet.

COUNSELOR: Well, if _____34_____ really _____35_____ about being an engineer, _____36_____ _____37_____ _____38_____ at least try. Then if _____39_____ don't like it, _____40_____ _____41_____ try something else.

TONY: All right. Do _____42_____ have any engineering classes in the mornings?

COUNSELOR: I _____43_____ _____44_____ . I'll check.

DISCUSSION

Work in small groups.

What can people do to increase their confidence?

20 Can't You Find an Apartment?

/t/ + *you* ⟶ **cha*

/t/ + *your*
/t/ + *you're* } ⟶ **cher*

Part 1 INTRODUCTION

CONVERSATION

Listen to each part of the conversation: first spoken with careful (slow) pronunciation; then spoken with relaxed (fast) pronunciation.

Careful (Slow) Pronunciation	Relaxed (Fast) Pronunciation

Careful (Slow) Pronunciation

HIRO: Can't you find an apartment?

SAM: No, I can't. The rent you have to pay is too high.

HIRO: You know, I have a friend who could try to get you an apartment.

SAM: You do?

HIRO: Yeah. He used to be a real estate salesperson.

SAM: Well, I don't want your friend to spend a lot of time on it.

HIRO: No problem. I'll tell him that you're new in town.

SAM: Great. Thank him in advance for me, okay?

HIRO: Sure. Tell me what you're looking for. Do you want a furnished or unfurnished apartment?

SAM: I don't know. Don't you think a furnished apartment would be expensive?

Relaxed (Fast) Pronunciation

HIRO: *Kant *cha find an apartment?

SAM: No, I *kant. The rent *cha *hafta pay is too high.

HIRO: *Ya know, I have a friend who could try *da *git *cha an apartment.

SAM: *Ya do?

HIRO: Yeah. He *useta be a real estate salesperson.

SAM: Well, I don't want *cher friend *ta spend a lot *a time on it.

HIRO: No problem. I'll tell *'im that *cher new in town.

SAM: Great. Thank *'im in advance *fer me, okay?

HIRO: Sure. Tell me what *cher *lookin' for. Do *ya want a furnished *er unfurnished apartment?

SAM: I *donno. Don't *cha think a furnished apartment would be expensive?

Listen to the entire conversation again, spoken with relaxed (fast) pronunciation.

COMPREHENSION

Answer these questions about the conversation.

1. What does Sam want?
2. Why can't Sam find what he wants?
3. Is Hiro's friend still a real estate salesperson?
4. Do you think Hiro's friend can help Sam? Explain.

Now, work with a partner and compare your answers.

PRACTICE

Close your book. You'll hear each part of the conversation spoken with relaxed pronunciation. Repeat each part using careful pronunciation.

Part 2 EXPANSION

COMPREHENSION

Listen to the conversation. The speakers use relaxed pronunciation.
Answer the questions.

1. How do the speakers introduce themselves?
2. What are other ways they could introduce themselves?
3. What are possible reasons that Sam doesn't want a roommate?
4. What does Mark know about Sam?
5. Do you think it will take a long time to find an apartment for Sam? Explain.
6. Do you think Sam has a job? Explain.

Work with a partner. Compare your answers. Listen again if necessary.

PRACTICE

Listen again. The conversation is spoken with relaxed pronunciation. Complete the sentences with the words you would hear if they were spoken with careful pronunciation. Then, listen once more and check your answers.

SAM: Hi. I'm Sam Trump.

MARK: How are _____ 1 _____ ? I'm Mark Baker.

SAM: Nice _____ 2 meet _____ 3 .

MARK: Nice _____ 4 meet _____ 5 , too.

SAM: My friend, Hiro, said that _____ 6 could help me. I _____ 7 _____ 8 find an apartment.

MARK: Sure. Hiro told me about _____ 9 . Do _____ 10 know _____ 11 _____ 12 _____ 13 for?

SAM: A one-bedroom apartment, but it's _____ 14 _____ 15 be cheap.

MARK: Then why _____ 16 _____ 17 try _____ 18 find a roommate? That would make it cheaper _____ 19 both _____ 20 _____ 21 .

SAM: _____ 22 _____ 23 _____ 24 is true, but right now, I don't _____ 25 _____ 26 have a roommate.

MARK: Okay. That reminds me. Hiro said that _____ 27 _____ 28 motel, there's a refrigerator _____ 29 a stove. _____ 30 _____ 31 _____ 32 _____ 33 _____ 34 find a place that has those, too, _____ 35 _____ 36 ?

SAM: I _____ 37 _____ 38 . I _____ 39 _____ 40 find a *cheap* apartment!

MARK: Okay. Don't worry. We'll find just _____ 41 _____ 42 _____ 43 _____ 44 sooner _____ 45 later.

DISCUSSION

Work in small groups.

What's the best way to find a place to live? Explain.

21 Could You Check My Sink?

/d/ + **you** ⟶ *ja

/d/ + **your** ⟶ *jer

Part 1 INTRODUCTION

CONVERSATION

Listen to each part of the conversation: first spoken with careful (slow) pronunciation; then spoken with relaxed (fast) pronunciation.

Careful (Slow) Pronunciation	Relaxed (Fast) Pronunciation
KARL: Jim, where are you? I knocked twice, but you didn't answer your door.	KARL: Jim, where are *ya? I knocked twice, but *cha didn't answer *yer door.
JIM: Karl! Could you come into the kitchen? Quick!	JIM: Karl! Could *ja come into the kitchen? Quick!
KARL: Oh, my gosh! Look at all of that water!	KARL: Oh, my gosh! Look at all *a that water!
JIM: Would you get me some towels?	JIM: Would *ja *git me some towels?
KARL: Sure. Did your pipe break?	KARL: Sure. Did *jer pipe break?
JIM: I can't hear you. What did you say?	JIM: I *kant hear *ya. What did *ja say?
KARL: I said, "Did your pipe break?"	KARL: I said, "Did *jer pipe break?"
JIM: Yes. Could you call your brother? He's a plumber, right?	JIM: Yes. Could *ja call *yer brother? He's a plumber, right?
KARL: I told you he moved last year, remember?	KARL: I told *ja he moved last year, remember?
JIM: Then could you call somebody else? This is an emergency!	JIM: Then could *ja call somebody else? This is an emergency!

Listen to the entire conversation again, spoken with relaxed (fast) pronunciation.

COMPREHENSION

Answer these questions about the conversation.

1. Where are Jim and Karl?
2. Do you think Karl is a neighbor? Explain.
3. What's Jim's problem?
4. What does he want to do?
5. Why is this an emergency?

Now, work with a partner and compare your answers.

PRACTICE

Close your book. You'll hear each part of the conversation spoken with relaxed pronunciation. Repeat each part using careful pronunciation.

Part 2 EXPANSION

COMPREHENSION

Listen to the conversation. The speakers use relaxed pronunciation. Answer the questions.

1. Is the plumber a man or a woman?
2. What's wrong with Jim's plumbing?
3. Why does Jim want the plumber to fix the plumbing cheaply?
4. Why doesn't Jim pay with a credit card?
5. What do you think will happen next?

Work with a partner. Compare your answers. Listen again if necessary.

PRACTICE

Listen again. The conversation is spoken with relaxed pronunciation. Complete the sentences with the words you would hear if they were spoken with careful pronunciation. Then, listen once more and check your answers.

HELEN: I think I found _____ leak.
                                               1

JIM: What did _____ say?
                           2

HELEN: I think I found _____ leak! I'm _____ _____
                              3   4   5
_____ _____ turn off _____ water!
        6   7   8
  When was the last time _____ had _____ pipes checked?
                               9   10

JIM: I had _____ checked maybe six _____ seven years ago.
                  11   12
  Are they that bad?

HELEN: _____ kitchen pipes _____ _____ be
                    13   14   15
  replaced, _____ _____ really need _____
                 16   17   18
  faucets changed. _____ _____ like me _____
                       19   20   21
  start now?

JIM: _____ _____ _____ change the pipes?
        22   23   24
_____ _____ just fix _____ ?
      25   26   27

HELEN: _____ _____ know there was a toy rabbit in
         28   29
_____ drain? I'm a plumber, not a magician.
      30

JIM: Well, I don't have much money. Would _____ do it as cheaply
                                              31
  as _____ _____ ?
       32   33

HELEN: Of course.

(Several hours later)

HELEN: That's _____ _____ be $347.63 _____ the
                  34   35   36
  new pipes _____ faucets.
                37

JIM: $347.63?

HELEN: Yes. Plus tax.

JIM: I only have $20. _____ _____ take a credit card? Most
        38   39
businesses take credit cards, right?

HELEN: I'm sorry. We don't take credit cards.

JIM: Oh. Then, we've got a problem!

DISCUSSION

Work in small groups.

Is a plumber an unusual job for a woman? What's an unusual job for a man? Explain.

22 Who Have You Asked to Fly the Plane?

Deletion of Initial /h/

Wh- question words + *have* ⟶ ***'ave***

Wh- question words + *has* ⟶ ***'as***

Wh- question words + *had* ⟶ ***'ad***

What have you can also become ***Whaddaya.*** A related form, ***Whadda,*** can be used when *What have* is followed by either *we* or *they*. EXAMPLE:

Whadda they done?

Part 1 INTRODUCTION

CONVERSATION

Listen to each part of the conversation: first spoken with careful (slow) pronunciation; then spoken with relaxed (fast) pronunciation.

Careful (Slow) Pronunciation

ELIZABETH: Well, hello! What have you been doing lately?

TOM: Oh, I've been hiking a lot. So, where has your sister been? I haven't seen her.

ELIZABETH: She's gone to Shanghai.

TOM: Shanghai? Why has she gone to Shanghai?

ELIZABETH: To visit some friends. So, who have you been hiking with?

TOM: Mostly my grandson. And how have your grandchildren been?

ELIZABETH: Great. I gave my granddaughter some skydiving lessons for her graduation.

Relaxed (Fast) Pronunciation

ELIZABETH: Well, hello! *Whaddaya been *doin' lately?

TOM: Oh, I've been *hikin' a lot. So, where *'as *yer sister been? I haven't seen *'er.

ELIZABETH: She's gone *ta Shanghai.

TOM: Shanghai? Why *'as she gone *ta Shanghai?

ELIZABETH: *Ta visit some friends. So, who *'ave *ya been *hikin' with?

TOM: Mostly my grandson. *'N' how *'ave *yer grandchildren been?

ELIZABETH: Great. I gave my granddaughter some skydiving lessons *fer *'er graduation.

TOM: Really? When had she become interested in skydiving?

ELIZABETH: Oh, a few months ago. We're, uh, doing it together.

TOM: You're jumping out of airplanes? What have your children said about that?

TOM: Really? When *'ad she become interested in skydiving?

ELIZABETH: Oh, a few months ago. We're, uh, *doin' it together.

TOM: *Yer *jumpin' out *a airplanes? *Whadda *yer children said about that?

Listen to the entire conversation again, spoken with relaxed (fast) pronunciation.

COMPREHENSION

Answer these questions about the conversation.

1. How well do you think Tom and Elizabeth know each other? Explain.
2. Where has Elizabeth's sister gone? Why?
3. How old do you think Tom and Elizabeth are? Why?
4. Do you think Elizabeth is too old to skydive? Explain.
5. Do you think Tom and Elizabeth are healthy? Explain.

Now, work with a partner and compare your answers.

PRACTICE

Close your book. You'll hear each part of the conversation spoken with relaxed pronunciation. Repeat each part using careful pronunciation.

Part 2 EXPANSION

COMPREHENSION

Listen to the conversation. The speakers use relaxed pronunciation.
Answer the questions.

1. Where are Robert and Elizabeth?
2. What do you think the relationship between them is?
3. Who didn't like airplanes?
4. Who took the skydiving class?
5. Did Elizabeth misunderstand something? Explain.
6. How often do you think Robert and Elizabeth see each other? Explain.

Work with a partner. Compare your answers. Listen again if necessary.

PRACTICE

Listen again. The conversation is spoken with relaxed pronunciation. Complete
the sentences with the words you would hear if they were spoken with careful
pronunciation. Then, listen once more and check your answers.

ELIZABETH: Robert!

ROBERT: Elizabeth! _____ _____ _____
             1   2   3

_____ at the tennis courts?
         4

ELIZABETH: I'm with a friend. So, how _____ _____ been?
                                              5   6

ROBERT: Great. How _____ *you* been?
                          7

ELIZABETH: Terrific. So, _____ _____ _____ been
                                8   9   10

_____ lately?
        11

ROBERT: Oh, _____ , _____ tennis . . . _____ I've
                   12   13   14

decided _____ go skydiving again.
                15

ELIZABETH: Really? When _____ _____ decided
                               16   17

_____ go skydiving?
          18

ROBERT: I'm _____ _____ go next week. _____ know,
                   19   20   21

when my wife was alive, she wouldn't even fly in airplanes. We _____
                                                                         22

_____ _____ _____ take trains everywhere.
        23   24   25

ELIZABETH: When my husband was alive, he wouldn't even watch skydiving on TV. So,

who _____ _____ decided _____ jump with?
           26   27   28

Our skydiving teacher?

ROBERT: No. My son.

ELIZABETH: Oh? Why _____ 29 _____ 30 decided _____ 31 do this? I thought _____ 32 didn't like skydiving.

ROBERT: Why _____ 33 _____ 34 thought that? He took the skydiving class after we did, _____ 35 _____ 36 loved it.

ELIZABETH: Why _____ 37 I thought that? I _____ 38 _____ 39 . I guess I misunderstood what _____ 40 told me in class.

ROBERT: Well, maybe _____ 41 didn't want me _____ 42 take the class at first, but when _____ 43 a son ever wanted _____ 44 father _____ 45 do something dangerous?

ELIZABETH: My children feel the same way. So, who _____ 46 _____ 47 asked _____ 48 fly the plane?

ROBERT: My younger daughter.

ELIZABETH: Jane? That's great. Where _____ 49 she been _____ 50 flying lessons?

ROBERT: At a local airport. She just got _____ 51 license. Do _____ 52 _____ 53 _____ 54 join us?

ELIZABETH: Sure. I'd love to.

DISCUSSION

Work in small groups.

Should elderly people date? Should they hike or skydive? Explain.

Could I Have an Appointment with Dr. Okamoto?

Deletion of Initial /h/

Subject	+	*have*	⟶ *'ave
Subject	+	*has*	⟶ *'as
Subject	+	*had*	⟶ *'ad
		haven't	⟶ *'aven't
		hasn't	⟶ *'asn't
		hadn't	⟶ *'adn't

Although Subject + *'ave can be pronounced *of, have doesn't reduce further to *a.

Part 1 INTRODUCTION

CONVERSATION

Listen to each part of the conversation: first spoken with careful (slow) pronunciation; then spoken with relaxed (fast) pronunciation.

Careful (Slow) Pronunciation	Relaxed (Fast) Pronunciation
RECEPTIONIST: Hello. Dr. Okamoto's office.	RECEPTIONIST: Hello. Dr. Okamoto's office.
TONY: This is Tony Lamotta. I have a terrible backache.	TONY: This is Tony Lamotta. I *'ave a terrible backache.
RECEPTIONIST: We have an opening tomorrow morning at 10:00.	RECEPTIONIST: We *'ave an opening tomorrow morning at 10:00.
TONY: I had to stay home from work today. You haven't got anything sooner?	TONY: I *'ad *ta stay home from work today. *Ya *'aven't got anything sooner?
RECEPTIONIST: Wait a minute. The doctor has a cancellation at 3:00 today. Can you come in then?	RECEPTIONIST: Wait a minute. The doctor *'as a cancellation at 3:00 today. *Kin *ya come in then?
TONY: She has an opening at 3:00? Thank you so much.	TONY: She *'as an opening at 3:00? Thank *ya so much.

RECEPTIONIST: You're welcome.
What kind of insurance do you have?

TONY: What kind of insurance do I have?

RECEPTIONIST: The doctors have a policy. If you don't have insurance, we can't bill you.

TONY: You mean, I'm going to have to pay her today? I hadn't planned for that.

RECEPTIONIST: *Yer welcome.
What kind *a insurance do *ya *'ave?

TONY: What kind *a insurance do I *'ave?

RECEPTIONIST: The doctors *'ave a policy. If *ya don't *'ave insurance, we *kant bill *ya.

TONY: *Ya mean, I'm *gonna *hafta pay *'er today? I *'adn't planned *fer that.

Listen to the entire conversation again, spoken with relaxed (fast) pronunciation.

COMPREHENSION

Answer these questions about the conversation.

1. What's Tony's problem?
2. When do they first offer him an appointment?
3. Why does he want an appointment sooner?
4. Do you think Tony has medical insurance? Explain.
5. What do you think the receptionist will say next?

Now, work with a partner and compare your answers.

PRACTICE

Close your book. You'll hear each part of the conversation spoken with relaxed pronunciation. Repeat each part using careful pronunciation.

Part 2 EXPANSION

COMPREHENSION

**Listen to the conversation. The speakers use relaxed pronunciation.
Answer the questions.**

1. Why do you think the doctor wants to listen to Tony's heart?
2. What's too cold for Tony?
3. How old is Tony?
4. How did Tony injure his back?
5. How old was Tony when he had his son?
6. What does Tony have to do to get better?

Work with a partner. Compare your answers. Listen again if necessary.

PRACTICE

**Listen again. The conversation is spoken with relaxed pronunciation. Complete
the sentences with the words you would hear if they were spoken with careful
pronunciation. Then, listen again and check your answers.**

DOCTOR OKAMOTO: Okay. Do _____ _____ any pain here?
                                 1   2

TONY: No. I _____ pain there last night, but not now.
                    3

DOCTOR: Please take off _____ shirt. I _____
                              4   5
_____ listen _____ _____ heart.
        6   7   8

TONY: Oh, my gosh!

DOCTOR: What's wrong? I _____ done anything yet. I'm just
                              9

_____ _____ _____ heart.
        10   11   12

TONY: Sorry. It's just cold.

DOCTOR: I'm really sorry. Sometimes, I forget _____ warm the stethoscope.
                                                      13

TONY: That's okay.

DOCTOR: Okay, now I want _____ _____ take a deep breath;
                               14   15
then, breathe out. Okay, good. We _____ a couple _____
                                          16   17
tests we need _____ do now. _____ _____
                     18   19   20
touch _____ toes _____ me?
             21   22

TONY: My toes? I _____ an injured back. I _____ even touch
                        23   24
my knees.

DOCTOR: How old are _____ , Tony?
                           25

TONY: Forty-nine. I _____ a birthday last month.
                           26

DOCTOR: Sometimes, as we _____ older, we _____ a little pain
                        27   28

    in the lower back. How is it when I touch _____ here?
                                                          29

TONY: Ouch! _____ _____ that all older people
                    30   31

    _____ this kind _____ pain?
         32   33

DOCTOR: No. Not as bad as this. How _____ _____ hurt
                                     34   35

    _____ back?
         36

TONY: _____ baseball with my eleven-year-old son. _____
       37   38

    _____ _____ practice.
         39   40

DOCTOR: Do _____ usually _____ this much pain?
               41   42

TONY: Well, no. We played _____ three hours. _____
                          43   44

    _____ a play-off game soon. _____ _____
         45   46   47

    been in the play-offs before.

DOCTOR: Well, no baseball _____ *you* _____ awhile.
                                 48   49

    _____ _____ _____ _____
        50   51   52   53

    _____ rest _____ a few weeks.
        54   55

DISCUSSION

Work in small groups.

Is it better to be a younger or an older parent? Explain.

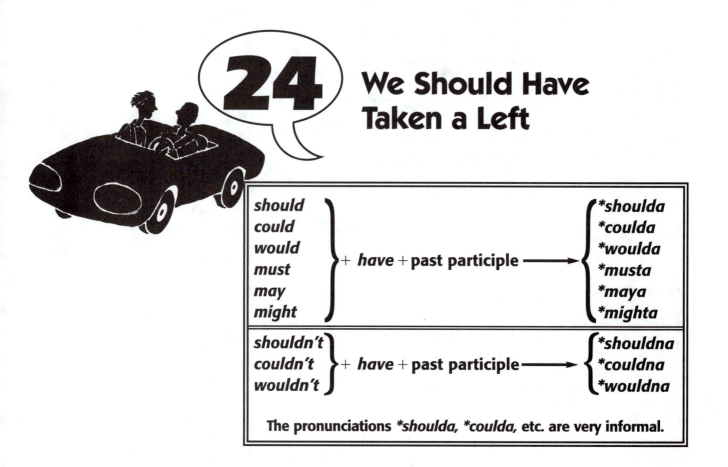

24 We Should Have Taken a Left

| should could would must may might | } + *have* + past participle ⟶ | { *shoulda *coulda *woulda *musta *maya *mighta |

| shouldn't couldn't wouldn't | } + *have* + past participle ⟶ | { *shouldna *couldna *wouldna |

The pronunciations *shoulda, *coulda, etc. are very informal.

Part 1 INTRODUCTION

CONVERSATION

Listen to each part of the conversation: first spoken with careful (slow) pronunciation; then spoken with relaxed (fast) pronunciation.

Careful (Slow) Pronunciation

HERMAN: Oh no! We should have been at Judy's house at a quarter of seven!

ZELDA: Well, you could have gotten directions ahead of time. That would have helped.

HERMAN: I must have been crazy to try to find her house out here.

ZELDA: Look, I think there may have been a gas station back there.

HERMAN: Zelda, we couldn't have driven by a gas station.

ZELDA: Well, I think we did. It might have been back a mile or so.

Relaxed (Fast) Pronunciation

HERMAN: Oh no! We *shoulda been at Judy's house at a quarter *a seven!

ZELDA: Well, *ya *coulda gotten directions ahead *a time. That *woulda helped.

HERMAN: I *musta been crazy *da try *da find *'er house out here.

ZELDA: Look, I think there *maya been a gas station back there.

HERMAN: Zelda, we *couldna driven by a gas station.

ZELDA: Well, I think we did. It *mighta been back a mile *er so.

HERMAN: No. I would have seen it.

ZELDA: Oh, Herman, you might have driven by the gas station while we were talking.

HERMAN: Where's the map? I knew I shouldn't have given the map to *you*.

ZELDA: Okay. So I forgot the map. We wouldn't have missed the gas station if you hadn't been talking so much.

HERMAN: No. I *woulda seen it.

ZELDA: Oh, Herman, *ya *mighta driven by the gas station while we were *talkin'.

HERMAN: Where's the map? I knew I *shouldna given the map *ta *you*.

ZELDA: Okay. So I forgot the map. We *wouldna missed the gas station if *ya *'adn't been *talkin' so much.

Listen to the entire conversation again, spoken with relaxed (fast) pronunciation.

COMPREHENSION

Answer these questions about the conversation.

1. What do you think the relationship between Zelda and Herman is?
2. What's their problem?
3. Do they have directions to Judy's house?
4. Why didn't they see the gas station?
5. Do they have a map? Explain.

Now, work with a partner and compare your answers.

PRACTICE

Close your book. You'll hear each part of the conversation spoken with relaxed pronunciation. Repeat each part using careful pronunciation.

Part 2 EXPANSION

COMPREHENSION

Listen to the conversation. The speakers use relaxed pronunciation.
Answer the questions.

1. How long do you think Zelda and Herman have been lost?
2. Should Herman have turned right at the market? Why or why not?
3. What are the directions to Lewis Street?
4. Why do you think they got lost?
5. Do you think Herman and Zelda have a good relationship? Explain.

Work with a partner. Compare your answers. Listen again if necessary.

PRACTICE

Listen again. The conversation is spoken with relaxed pronunciation. Complete
the sentences with the words you would hear if they were spoken with careful
pronunciation. Then, listen once more and check your answers.

ZELDA: We're lost. We're *really* lost. Maybe we _____ (1) _____ (2)

taken a left on Clark Street.

HERMAN: We _____ (3) _____ (4) done that. _____ (5)
_____ (6) see the construction in front _____ (7) the entrance
_____ (8) the street?

ZELDA: Oh, Herman, what construction? If there _____ (9) been any construction,
I _____ (10) _____ (11) seen it. It _____ (12)
_____ (13) been another street.

HERMAN: It _____ (14) _____ (15) been. I _____ (16)
_____ (17) .

ZELDA: Turn right! Turn right at the market!

HERMAN: Okay, okay!

(Ten minutes later)

ZELDA: I think we need _____ (18) find a gas station. There _____ (19)
_____ (20) been one back there somewhere. There _____ (21)
_____ (22) been one back a mile _____ (23) so.

HERMAN: I knew we _____ (24) _____ (25) turned right at the market.
Why were _____ (26) _____ (27) at me, "Turn right! Turn right!"?

(Ten minutes later)

GAS STATION ATTENDANT: _____ I help _____ ?
                              28   29

ZELDA: Yes. We're lost.

HERMAN: I think we _____ _____ turned at the wrong
                              30   31

street. We're _____ _____ Lewis Street.
                      32   33

ATTENDANT: _____ _____ _____ turned left on
                    34   35   36

Clark Street. Then _____ _____ _____ seen
                            37   38   39

Lewis Street on _____ left.
                        40

ZELDA: Herman, _____ _____ _____ driven right
                        41   42   43

by it _____ not seen it.
              44

HERMAN: I _____ _____ done that, could I?
                  45   46

ATTENDANT: The street sign _____ _____ been down. Anyway,
                                    47   48

take a right out _____ the gas station. Go straight _____
                          49   50

about ten miles. Then turn left on Clark Street. Lewis Street will be on

_____ left.
        51

HERMAN: Thank you. (*to Zelda*) Zelda, next time, don't yell at me. We _____
                                                                                52

_____ been driving around _____ around if
        53   54

_____ _____ yelled at me. _____
        55   56   57

made me nervous.

DISCUSSION

Work in small groups.

What should people do when they're lost? What do you usually do? Explain.

25 What Are You Doing to My Hair?

What are you	⟶	***Whacha***

Whacha is more informal than *Whaddaya*.
Whacha is occasionally used for *What do you.*

Part 1 INTRODUCTION

CONVERSATION

Listen to each part of the conversation: first spoken with careful (slow) pronunciation; then spoken with relaxed (fast) pronunciation.

Careful (Slow) Pronunciation	Relaxed (Fast) Pronunciation
BILL: What are you doing this afternoon?	BILL: *Whacha *doin' this afternoon?
GEORGETTE: I'm going to go to my cousin's new hair salon. He's going to do my hair.	GEORGETTE: I'm *gonna go *da my cousin's new hair salon. He's *gonna do my hair.
BILL: What are you going to do to your hair? I love your hair.	BILL: *Whacha *gonna do *da *yer hair? I love *yer hair.
GEORGETTE: I don't know. Don't you think I should change my hairstyle?	GEORGETTE: I *donno. Don't *cha think I should change my hairstyle?
BILL: What do you want to do that for? Our hairstyles are the same.	BILL: *Whacha *wanna do that for? Our hairstyles are the same.
GEORGETTE: I see what you mean. But what are you going to do about finding a job?	GEORGETTE: I see what *cha mean. But *whacha *gonna do about *findin' a job?
BILL: I don't know. What do you think I should do?	BILL: I *donno. *Whaddaya think I should do?
GEORGETTE: Well, maybe we should try to look a little more professional.	GEORGETTE: Well, maybe we should try *da look a little more professional.
BILL: Why?	BILL: Why?
GEORGETTE: Well, we're both looking for jobs, and we need to change our "look."	GEORGETTE: Well, we're both *lookin' *fer jobs, *'n' we need *ta change our "look."

Listen to the entire conversation again, spoken with relaxed (fast) pronunciation.

COMPREHENSION

Answer these questions about the conversation.

1. What do you think the relationship between Bill and Georgette is? Explain.
2. Do Bill and Georgette like their hairstyles? Explain.
3. What does Georgette think Bill should do to get a job?
4. Do you think this is a good idea? Explain.
5. How old do you think Bill and Georgette are? Why?

Now, work with a partner and compare your answers.

PRACTICE

Close your book. You'll hear each part of the conversation spoken with relaxed pronunciation. Repeat each part using careful pronunciation.

Part 2 EXPANSION

COMPREHENSION

Listen to the conversation. The speakers use relaxed pronunciation. Answer the questions.

1. Did Georgette's cousin cut off a lot of hair? Explain.
2. Why do you think George says, "Hair grows so fast"?
3. Do you think Georgette should have let George continue to cut her hair? Explain.
4. What do you think George's biggest problem is?
5. Would you go to George to get your hair cut? Explain.

Work with a partner. Compare your answers. Listen again if necessary.

PRACTICE

Listen again. The conversation is spoken with relaxed pronunciation. Complete
the sentences with the words you would hear if they were spoken with careful
pronunciation. Then, listen once more and check your answers.

GEORGETTE: George, _____ _____ _____
  1   2   3
_____ back there?
  4

GEORGE: I'm _____ _____ _____ told me
  5   6   7
_____ do. I'm _____ _____ hair.
  8   9   10

GEORGETTE: I didn't say _____ cut it! I said _____ *trim* it. Look,
  11   12
_____ my cousin, _____ I love _____ , but are
  13   14   15
_____ sure _____ know _____
  16   17   18
_____ _____ ?
  19   20

GEORGE: Don't worry. Short hair is very popular this year.

GEORGETTE: How much did _____ cut off?
  21

GEORGE: Not much. Just six _____ seven inches.
  22

GEORGETTE: Oh. _____ _____ _____
  23   24   25
_____ off the top now?
  26

GEORGE: About four _____ five inches.
  27

GEORGETTE: I told _____ *two* inches!
  28

GEORGE: Oh, hair grows so fast. _____ _____
  29   30
_____ look great.
  31

GEORGETTE: I _____ _____ . _____
  32   33   34
_____ _____ _____ _____ do
  35   36   37   38
_____ the bangs?
  39

GEORGE: I've _____ _____ even _____ out a little.
  40   41   42

GEORGETTE: _____ _____ _____
  43   44   45
_____ now?
  46

GEORGE: I'm just _____ this big . . . piece . . . here. _____ don't
                        47   48

need _____ worry. Hair grows so fast.
           49

GEORGETTE: Well, _____ _____ _____ decided
                    50   51   52

_____ do _____ the sides _____ my hair?
    53   54   55

Maybe it'll look better when it's finished.

GEORGE: It *is* finished.

DISCUSSION

Work in small groups.

How should people look when they go on a job interview or start a new job? Which things are the most important? Why?

26 Give Me a Paintbrush

let me ⟶ *lemme
give me ⟶ *gimme

*Lemme and *gimme are very informal.

Part 1 INTRODUCTION

CONVERSATION

Listen to each part of the conversation: first spoken with careful (slow) pronunciation; then spoken with relaxed (fast) pronunciation.

Careful (Slow) Pronunciation	Relaxed (Fast) Pronunciation
DAN: My brother's going to give me some paint for my birthday.	DAN: My brother's *gonna *gimme some paint *fer my birthday.
LISA: Let me guess. You're finally going to paint your living room.	LISA: *Lemme guess. *Yer finally *gonna paint *cher living room.
DAN: Yeah. Can you give me some advice? I can't decide on a color.	DAN: Yeah. *Kin *ya *gimme some advice? I *kant decide on a color.
LISA: Well, I used to work in a paint store. Let me see the color samples.	LISA: Well, I *useta work in a paint store. *Lemme see the color samples.
DAN: Okay. I have to choose from these.	DAN: Okay. I *hafta choose from these.
LISA: No problem. Give me the samples and tell me what colors you like.	LISA: No problem. *Gimme the samples *'n' tell me what colors *ya like.
DAN: Well, let me see the grays. What do you think about dark gray?	DAN: Well, *lemme see the grays. *Whaddaya think about dark gray?
LISA: It's too dark for me. Let me show you this light brown. Do you like it?	LISA: It's too dark *fer me. *Lemme show *ya this light brown. Do *ya like it?

86 Chapter 26

DAN: I don't know. Give me a
minute to think about it.

LISA: Did you see this beautiful
yellow? We should have looked at
this one first.

DAN: I *donno. *Gimme a
minute *ta think about it.

LISA: Did *ja see this beautiful
yellow? We *shoulda looked at
this one first.

Listen to the entire conversation again, spoken with relaxed (fast) pronunciation.

COMPREHENSION

Answer these questions about the conversation.

1. What do you think the relationship between Dan and Lisa is? Explain.
2. Why do you think Dan is getting paint for his birthday?
3. Who do you think knows more about choosing colors to paint a room, Dan or Lisa? Explain.
4. What do you think is the best color to paint Dan's living room? Why?

Now, work with a partner and compare your answers.

PRACTICE

Close your book. You'll hear each part of the conversation spoken with relaxed pronunciation. Repeat each part using careful pronunciation.

Part 2 EXPANSION

COMPREHENSION

Listen to the conversation. The speakers use relaxed pronunciation. Answer the questions.

1. What's the relationship between Dan and Leonard?
2. What are the steps in painting a room?
3. Does Leonard know how to paint a room? Explain.
4. Why do you think Dan felt that Leonard was a *house* painter?
5. Do you think Leonard made a lot of money as an artist? Why or why not?

Work with a partner. Compare your answers. Listen again if necessary.

PRACTICE

Listen again. The conversation is spoken with relaxed pronunciation. Complete the sentences with the words you would hear if they were spoken with careful pronunciation. Then, listen once more and check your answers.

DAN: I _____ _____ paint our living room, Leonard. Do
        ₁   ₂

_____ know how _____ paint?
        ₃   ₄

LEONARD: Do I know how _____ paint? Do *I* know how _____
                        ₅   ₆

paint? Now, I sell computers _____ pay my half _____ our
                            ₇   ₈

rent, but I _____ _____ be a painter.
            ₉   ₁₀

DAN: _____ did? Great! I _____ _____ anything
        ₁₁   ₁₂   ₁₃

about painting.

LEONARD: Here, Dan. _____ _____ open that paint can.
                      ₁₄   ₁₅

DAN: Oh, my gosh! _____ spilled it!
                    ₁₆

LEONARD: _____ _____ a rag. I'll clean it up. See? No problem.
            ₁₇   ₁₈

_____ _____ a paintbrush. Let's _____ started.
        ₁₉   ₂₀   ₂₁

DAN: Shouldn't we cover the furniture with sheets first? We don't _____
                                                                    ₂₂

_____ _____ paint on our furniture.
        ₂₃   ₂₄

LEONARD: Yes. Good idea. _____ _____ help _____ .
                          ₂₅   ₂₆   ₂₇

_____ _____ the other corner _____
        ₂₈   ₂₉   ₃₀

the sheet.

(A few minutes later)

LEONARD: _____ _____ a paintbrush. Let's
            31   32

_____ started.
   33

DAN: But, shouldn't we sand the walls first?

LEONARD: Sand the walls? Good idea.

(Thirty minutes later)

LEONARD: Okay. We sanded the walls. What a great idea! Now, _____
                                                              34

_____ a paintbrush. _____ _____ paint this
   35   36   37

wall. *You* paint the other one.

DAN: Sure. _____ the painter.
          38

(An hour later)

DAN: My wall's finished. _____ _____ see _____ .
                                39   40   41

LEONARD: There it is. Isn't it beautiful?

DAN: _____ said _____ were a painter! _____
         42   43   44

_____ _____ painted on _____ wall?
   45   46   47

LEONARD: Cheese. The yellow paint made me think _____ cheese.
                                                              48

_____ _____ explain. I was never a *house*
   49   50

painter. I _____ _____ be an *artist*.
               51   52

DISCUSSION

Work in small groups.

What are the best colors for a room where you spend a lot of time? Explain.

27 I Couldn't Take the Test Because I Was Sick

Deletion of Syllables:

about	→	*****'bout*
because	→	*****'cause*
come on	→	*****c'mon*

*****'Bout, *****'cause,** and *****c'mon** are very informal.

Part 1 INTRODUCTION

CONVERSATION

Listen to each part of the conversation: first spoken with careful (slow) pronunciation; then spoken with relaxed (fast) pronunciation.

Careful (Slow) Pronunciation	Relaxed (Fast) Pronunciation
JUAN: Can you give me a ride to school?	JUAN: *Kin *ya *gimme a ride *ta school?
MRS. RODRIGUEZ: I can't because I have to finish a report before I leave.	MRS. RODRIGUEZ: I *kant *'cause I *hafta finish a report before I leave.
JUAN: Well, how long is it going to take you?	JUAN: Well, how long is it *gonna take *ya?
MRS. RODRIGUEZ: Oh, about thirty or forty minutes.	MRS. RODRIGUEZ: Oh, *'bout thirty *er forty minutes.
JUAN: Come on, Mom. I don't want to be late for my makeup test.	JUAN: *C'mon, Mom. I don't *wanna be late *fer my makeup test.
MRS. RODRIGUEZ: Makeup test? What are you talking about?	MRS. RODRIGUEZ: Makeup test? *Whaddaya *talkin' *bout?
JUAN: I forgot to tell you. I missed a test because I was sick.	JUAN: I forgot *ta tell *ya. I missed a test *'cause I was sick.
MRS. RODRIGUEZ: You missed the test when you had the flu?	MRS. RODRIGUEZ: *Ya missed the test when *ya *'ad the flu?
JUAN: Yeah. Mom, can you give me some money, too? I won't have time to make my lunch now—	JUAN: Yeah. Mom, *kin *ya *gimme some money, too? I won't have time *ta make my lunch now—

MRS. RODRIGUEZ: —because of
the makeup test. Here's your
money. Come on. Let's go.

MRS. RODRIGUEZ: —*'cause *a
the makeup test. Here's *yer
money. *C'mon. Let's go.

Listen to the entire conversation again, spoken with relaxed (fast) pronunciation.

COMPREHENSION

Answer these questions about the conversation.

1. Why is Juan taking a makeup test?
2. Why does he want a ride to school?
3. Why does he need money?
4. What's Juan's last name?
5. What time of day do you think it is? Explain.
6. Do you think his mother should drive him to school? Explain.

Now, work with a partner and compare your answers.

PRACTICE

Close your book. You'll hear each part of the conversation spoken with relaxed pronunciation. Repeat each part using careful pronunciation.

Part 2 EXPANSION

COMPREHENSION

Listen to the conversation. The speakers use relaxed pronunciation. Answer the questions.

1. Where are Juan and Martin? Explain.
2. What are they going to do? Why?
3. What does Martin have to do to get a scholarship? Why?
4. Does Juan work? Why or why not?

Work with a partner. Compare your answers. Listen again if necessary.

PRACTICE

Listen again. The conversation is spoken with relaxed pronunciation. Complete the sentences with the words you would hear if they were spoken with careful pronunciation. Then, listen once more and check your answers.

MARTIN: Hi, Juan. Where are _____ _____ ?
                                                      1   2

JUAN: Well, I _____ _____ take a makeup test in our history
                           3   4

class _____ I was sick.
                 5

MARTIN: A lot _____ people missed the test. _____
                           6   7

_____ . I _____ _____ take it, too.
        8   9   10

JUAN: *You* missed it, too?

MARTIN: Yeah.

JUAN: How long do _____ think it'll take?
                                    11

MARTIN: _____ an hour.
                       12

JUAN: So, did _____ study?
                          13

MARTIN: I studied a lot. I _____ _____ _____
                                          14   15   16

an "A" in this class _____ I _____ _____
                                 17   18   19

_____ a scholarship. I _____ _____ go
        20   21   22

_____ graduate school.
        23

JUAN: I _____ a scholarship, Martin, but I still _____
                 24   25

_____ work _____ college is so expensive.
        26   27

MARTIN: _____ right. I've been _____ _____
                     28   29   30

_____ a year. If I _____ a scholarship, I'll still
        31   32

92   Chapter 27

_____ _____ work, but my parents won't _____
₃₃ ₃₄ ₃₅
_____ pay so much. Anyway, _____ _____ .
₃₆ ₃₇ ₃₈
Let's go. We're _____ _____ be late.
₃₉ ₄₀

JUAN: *You* go ahead. I've _____ _____ go _____
₄₁ ₄₂ ₄₃

my locker _____ I've _____ _____
₄₄ ₄₅ ₄₆

_____ some books.
₄₇

MARTIN: How long will _____ be?
₄₈

JUAN: _____ ten minutes.
₄₉

MARTIN: Okay. See _____ at the test.
₅₀

JUAN: Yeah. See _____ there.
₅₁

DISCUSSION

Work in small groups.

Who do you think should pay for a student's education? Explain.

28 Been to the Circus Lately?

Deletion of Words in Questions:

Do you want some . . . ⟶ *Want some . . .*

Are you going to see . . . ⟶ **Gonna see . . .*

Would you like to . . . ⟶ *Like to . . .*

Have you seen the . . . ⟶ *Seen the . . .*

These forms are very informal. We can delete the first one or two words of these questions. EXAMPLES:

Do you want some popcorn?
*Ya want some popcorn? OR *Want* some popcorn?

Have you seen any good movies?
*Ya seen any good movies? OR *Seen* any good movies?

Part 1 INTRODUCTION

CONVERSATION

Listen to each part of the conversation: first spoken with careful (slow) pronunciation; then spoken with relaxed (fast) pronunciation.

Careful (Slow) Pronunciation	Relaxed (Fast) Pronunciation
PAUL: Have you seen any good shows for kids lately?	PAUL: Seen any good shows *fer kids lately?
ANNE: Are you thinking about your son, Joey?	ANNE: *Ya *thinkin' *'bout *cher son, Joey?
PAUL: Yeah. Do you know what I did last week?	PAUL: Yeah. Know what I did last week?
ANNE: What did you do?	ANNE: What did *ja do?
PAUL: I got tickets to see the circus. Have you been to the circus lately?	PAUL: I got tickets *ta see the circus. Been *ta the circus lately?
ANNE: No. I've never been to the circus.	ANNE: No. I've never been *ta the circus.
PAUL: Would you like to go with us? I really want Joey to meet you.	PAUL: Like *ta go with us? I really want Joey *da meet *cha.

ANNE: Sounds great. Are you going to leave early?

PAUL: I was thinking about leaving around 9:00 A.M. Do you want to leave earlier?

ANNE: No, that's fine. Do you need me to bring anything?

ANNE: Sounds great. *Ya *gonna leave early?

PAUL: I was *thinkin' *'bout *leavin' around 9:00 A.M. *Ya *wanna leave earlier?

ANNE: No, that's fine. Need me *da bring anything?

Listen to the entire conversation again, spoken with relaxed (fast) pronunciation.

COMPREHENSION

Answer these questions about the conversation.

1. What do you think the relationship between Paul and Anne is? Explain.
2. Do you think they've known each other a long time? Explain.
3. Where are they planning to go? Why?
4. When do you think the performance is: in the morning, afternoon, or evening? Explain.

Now, work with a partner and compare your answers.

PRACTICE

Close your book. You'll hear each part of the conversation spoken with relaxed pronunciation. Repeat each part using careful pronunciation.

Part 2 EXPANSION

COMPREHENSION

Listen to the conversation. The speakers use relaxed pronunciation. Answer the questions.

1. How old do you think Joey is? Why?
2. Do you think Joey likes Anne at first? Explain.
3. Do you think Joey's mother really said he shouldn't see the tigers? Explain.
4. Do you think Joey's behaving badly? Explain.
5. Do you think Joey's feelings about Anne change? Explain.

Work with a partner. Compare your answers. Listen again if necessary.

PRACTICE

Listen again. The conversation is spoken with relaxed pronunciation. Complete the sentences with the words you would hear if they were spoken with careful pronunciation. Then, listen once more and check your answers.

PAUL: Anne, this is Joey. Joey, I _____ _____
                                                   1   2
_____ meet Anne. We're _____ _____
              3   4   5
have a great time today.

ANNE: Nice _____ _____ _____ .
                        6   7   8
JOEY: Hi.

ANNE: This is my first time at the circus _____ I'm really excited.
                                                              9
(_____ _____) _____ _____
          10   11   12   13
see the elephants, Joey?

JOEY: No.

ANNE: Okay. _____ like animals, _____ _____ ?
                        14   15   16
JOEY: I _____ _____ .
                   17   18
PAUL: Joey.

ANNE: It's okay, Paul. (*to Joey*) (_____ _____)
                                                    19   20
_____ _____ have a hot dog?
          21   22
JOEY: No, thanks.

ANNE: Well, (_____ _____) _____ the tigers
                          23   24   25
before? They're really exciting _____ watch. _____
                                            26   27
_____ . I'll take _____ _____ see
          28   29   30
_____ .
          31

JOEY: My mom doesn't want me _____ see the tigers.
                                                 32

ANNE: But this is the circus.

PAUL: (to Anne) He's just a little shy. Give _____ some time.
                                                            33
   (to Joey) (_____ _____) _____ what I
                        34   35   36
   _____ _____ do?
           37   38

JOEY: What?

PAUL: I _____ _____ see the clowns.
                   39   40

JOEY: Yeah! Let's see the clowns! (to Anne) (_____) _____
                                                              41   42
   _____ _____ come with us?
           43   44

ANNE: (_____ _____) _____ me
                    45   46   47
   _____ come with _____ ?
           48   49

JOEY: Yeah.

DISCUSSION

Work in small groups.

Do you think a husband and wife should stay married forever if they have children?
Explain.

29 Where Are Your Extra-Large Hats?

Unusual Contractions:

What are	⟶	**What're*
What will	⟶	**What'll*
Where are	⟶	**Where're*
Where will	⟶	**Where'll*
Why are	⟶	**Why're*
Why will	⟶	**Why'll*

Part 1 INTRODUCTION

CONVERSATION

Listen to each part of the conversation: first spoken with careful (slow) pronunciation; then spoken with relaxed (fast) pronunciation.

Careful (Slow) Pronunciation	Relaxed (Fast) Pronunciation
HENRY: What are you doing?	HENRY: *What're *ya *doin'?
FRANK: I'm looking in the phone book for stores that sell extra-large hats.	FRANK: I'm *lookin' in the phone book *fer stores that sell extra-large hats.
HENRY: Why are you looking for a hat?	HENRY: *Why're *ya *lookin' *fer a hat?
FRANK: I'm going to go to a soccer game. If I can't find a hat, what will I wear to protect my head?	FRANK: I'm *gonna go *da a soccer game. If I *kant find a hat, *what'll I wear *ta protect my head?
HENRY: Why will you need an *extra-large* hat?	HENRY: *Why'll *ya need an *extra-large* hat?
FRANK: Because I have a really big head.	FRANK: *'Cause I *'ave a really big head.
HENRY: No, you don't. Anyway, where will you be sitting?	HENRY: No, *ya don't. Anyway, *where'll *ya be *sittin'?
FRANK: In the stands. In the sun. Where are some good hat stores?	FRANK: In the stands. In the sun. *Where're some good hat stores?

HENRY: I don't know, but why are you doing this now? You should have done it a few days ago.

FRANK: What are you talking about? I started looking for a hat last week.

HENRY: I *donno, but *why're *ya *doin' this now? *Ya *shoulda done it a few days ago.

FRANK: *What're *ya *talkin' *'bout? I started *lookin' *fer a hat last week.

Listen to the entire conversation again, spoken with relaxed (fast) pronunciation.

COMPREHENSION

Answer these questions about the conversation.

1. What do you think the relationship between Frank and Henry is? Explain.
2. What's Frank looking for in the telephone book?
3. Why does he need an extra-large hat?
4. When did Frank start looking for a hat?

Now, work with a partner and compare your answers.

PRACTICE

Close your book. You'll hear each part of the conversation spoken with relaxed pronunciation. Repeat each part using careful pronunciation.

Part 2 EXPANSION _____

COMPREHENSION

Listen to the conversation. The speakers use relaxed pronunciation. Answer the questions.

1. What's Frank trying to do?
2. Why doesn't Frank call one of the departments directly?
3. How many departments does Frank talk to?
4. Why does each department transfer him to another department?
5. How do you think Frank feels at the end of the telephone call? Why?

Work with a partner. Compare your answers. Listen again if necessary.

PRACTICE

Listen again. The conversation is spoken with relaxed pronunciation. Complete the sentences with the words you would hear if they were spoken with careful pronunciation. Then, listen once more and check your answers.

RECORDING: LaPorte Department Store. _____ our main directory,

　　　　　　　　　　　　　　　　　　　　　1

please press 1 now. Thank you. _____ speak _____ an

　　　　　　　　　　　　　　　　　　2　　　　　　　　　　　　　　3

operator, please stay on the line. Thank you.

OPERATOR: May I help _____ ?

　　　　　　　　　　　　　　4

FRANK: Yes. _____ _____ I find extra-large hats?

　　　　　　　　5　　　　　　　　　　　6

OPERATOR: I'll _____ _____ _____ Men's Clothing.

　　　　　　　7　　　　　　　　8　　　　　　　　9

FRANK: Thank you.

MEN'S CLOTHING: Men's Clothing. _____ I help _____ ?

　　　　　　　　　　　　　　　　　　10　　　　　　　　　　11

FRANK: Yes. _____ _____ _____ extra-large hats?

　　　　　　12　　　　　　　13　　　　　　　14

MEN'S CLOTHING: Extra-large hats? Hmm. I'm _____ _____

　　　　　　　　　　　　　　　　　　　　　　　　　15　　　　　　　　　16

_____ _____ transfer _____

　　　17　　　　　　　18　　　　　　　　　　　　　19

_____ Accessories.

　　　20

ACCESSORIES: Accessories. _____ I help _____ ?

　　　　　　　　　　　　21　　　　　　　　　22

FRANK: Uh, _____ _____ I find extra-large hats?

　　　　　　23　　　　　　　24

ACCESSORIES: Extra-large hats? _____ _____ transfer

　　　　　　　　　　　　　25　　　　　　　　26

_____ _____ Sporting Goods.

　　　27　　　　　　　28

FRANK: Thanks.

SPORTING GOODS: Sporting Goods. May I help _____ ?

　　　　　　　　　　　　　　　　　　　　29

FRANK: _____ _____ _____ operators
              30   31   32
transferring me all over the store?

SPORTING GOODS: I'm sorry, sir. _____ _____
                                33   34
_____ _____ for?
     35   36

FRANK: Extra-large hats. _____ _____ I find _____ ?
                   37   38   39

SPORTING GOODS: I'm sorry. I'll _____ _____ transfer
                         40   41
_____ _____ Men's Clothing.
     42   43

FRANK: What? _____ _____ I _____
               44   45   46
_____ be transferred _____ Men's Clothing? I just
     47   48
talked _____ _____ . I've been _____
            49   50   51
_____ people all over _____ store. _____
     52   53   54
_____ I _____ _____ do
     55   56   57
_____ find an extra-large hat?
     58

SPORTING GOODS: We don't sell extra-large hats in my department. I'm really sorry.

I'll transfer _____ _____ the operator. Maybe she
                  59   60
_____ help _____ .
     61   62

RECORDING: Our lines are all busy. _____ call is important
                           63
_____ us. Please stay on the line.
     64

FRANK: I got disconnected! I _____ believe it!
                   65

DISCUSSION

Work in small groups.

Is the telephone the best way to get information? Why or why not? What are other ways to get information about department stores? Explain.

30 When Will Your TV Program Be Over?

Unusual Contractions:

Who are	⟶	*Who're
Who will	⟶	*Who'll
When are	⟶	*When're
When will	⟶	*When'll
How are	⟶	*How're
How will	⟶	*How'll

Part 1 INTRODUCTION

CONVERSATION

Listen to each part of the conversation: first spoken with careful (slow) pronunciation; then spoken with relaxed (fast) pronunciation.

Careful (Slow) Pronunciation

ELLEN: How will we get this box inside of the house? We'll have to ask the kids to help us.

DAVID: How are they going to help us? They're not even home.

ELLEN: Oh, I forgot. So, when will we tell them your parents gave them their spare TV?

DAVID: Come on. Let's get it inside. We'll talk about that later.

ELLEN: Who will set up the TV? I don't know how to do that.

DAVID: You don't? What do we need to do?

ELLEN: It's in a box. We've got to ask somebody.

DAVID: Who are we going to ask?

Relaxed (Fast) Pronunciation

ELLEN: *How'll we *git this box inside *a the house? We'll *hafta ask the kids *ta help us.

DAVID: *How're they *gonna help us? They're not even home.

ELLEN: Oh, I forgot. So, *when'll we tell *'em *yer parents gave *'em their spare TV?

DAVID: *C'mon. Let's *git it inside. We'll talk *'bout that later.

ELLEN: *Who'll set up the TV? I *donno how *da do that.

DAVID: *Ya don't? *Whadda we need *ta do?

ELLEN: It's in a box. We've *gotta ask somebody.

DAVID: *Who're we *gonna ask?

ELLEN: The kids. After all,
Joan's going to be fifteen and
Keith is almost sixteen.

DAVID: The kids? When are
kids shown how to set up the
cable and all of that?

ELLEN: The kids. After all,
Joan's *gonna be fifteen *'n'
Keith is almost sixteen.

DAVID: The kids? *When're
kids shown how *da set up the
cable *'n' all *a that?

Listen to the entire conservation again, spoken with relaxed (fast) pronunciation.

COMPREHENSION

Answer these questions about the conversation.

1. What do you think the relationship between Ellen and David is?
2. Is the TV new or old? Explain.
3. What do you know about Joan and Keith?
4. Do Ellen and David both have confidence in their children? Explain.

Now, work with a partner and compare your answers.

PRACTICE

Close your book. You'll hear each part of the conversation spoken with relaxed pronunciation. Repeat each part using careful pronunciation.

Part 2 EXPANSION

COMPREHENSION

Listen to the conversation. The speakers use relaxed pronunciation. Answer the questions.

1. Who set up the TV?
2. Why do you think Keith wants to watch *Accountants from Mars?*
3. Why do you think Joan wants to watch *Teen Issues?*
4. Why do Joan and Keith have to agree on a program?
5. What did they finally agree to watch? Why?
6. Do you think Joan and Keith get along well? Explain.

Work with a partner. Compare your answers. Listen again if necessary.

PRACTICE

Listen again. The conversation is spoken with relaxed pronunciation. Complete the sentences with the words you would hear if they were spoken with careful pronunciation. Then, listen once more and check your answers.

JOAN: I'm the one who set up the TV, Keith. _____ _____
            1   2

_____ _____ _____ be done with
        3   4   5

_____ program?
        6

KEITH: Shh! I'm _____ *Accountants from Mars.*
                        7

JOAN: So. _____ _____ it be over? I _____
                    8   9   10

_____ watch something.
        11

KEITH: _____ _____ _____ _____
              12   13   14   15

_____ watch?
        16

JOAN: *Teen Issues.*

KEITH: Oh, no! I'm not _____ _____ watch a bunch
                                17   18

_____ girls _____ _____ how they feel.
        19   20   21

JOAN: _____ know, we're _____ _____ share
              22   23   24

this TV.

KEITH: _____ _____ we _____
              25   26   27

_____ do that?
        28

JOAN: _____ could watch *Teen Issues.*
              29

KEITH: No. I'd rather _____ surgery. *You* could watch *Accountants*
                                30

from Mars.

JOAN: No. I really couldn't.

KEITH: Well, I offered _____ a compromise.
                          31

JOAN: _____ _____ _____ _____ ?
          32   33   34   35
That was no compromise.

KEITH: Look, we _____ _____ agree on a program.
                          36   37

JOAN: _____ _____ we do that?
              38   39

KEITH: Well, I guess we've _____ _____ find something we
                                      40   41
both like.

JOAN: Yeah, right. _____ _____ decide if we _____
                            42   43   44
agree?

KEITH: We've _____ _____ agree.
                      45   46

JOAN: Okay. (_____ _____) _____ Music Fever?
                      47   48   49

KEITH: Is that the one where they let all _____ these people with
                                                    50
terrible voices sing?

JOAN: Yeah.

KEITH: I love that show!

DISCUSSION

Work in small groups.

What's your favorite television program? Why?

Test Yourself

Each of the following ten tests gives additional practice with reduced forms that are often confused. Take each test after you complete the chapter that is mentioned. When you finish *Whaddaya Say?* take all ten tests together to reinforce your understanding of spoken English.

Test 1: Do *ya/Are *ya   (Do after Chapter 5.)

Listen to the short conversation. Which do you hear: *Do you* or *Are you?* Circle the correct words.

1. Do you	Are you
2. Do you	Are you
3. Do you	Are you
4. Do you	Are you
5. Do you	Are you

Test 2: *wanna/*gonna   (Do after Chapter 9.)

Listen to the short conversation. Which do you hear: *want to* or *going to?* Circle the correct words.

1. want to	going to
2. want to	going to
3. want to	going to
4. want to	going to
5. want to	going to
want to	going to

Test 3: *kin/*kant   (Do after Chapter 10.)

Listen to the short conversation. Which do you hear: *can* or *can't?* Circle the correct word.

1. can	can't
2. can	can't
can	can't
3. can	can't
can	can't
4. can	can't
5. can	can't
can	can't

Test 4: *hafta/*hasta   (Do after Chapter 14.)

Listen to the short conversation. Which do you hear: *have to* or *has to*? Circle the correct words.

1. have to	has to	
2. have to	has to	
have to	has to	
3. have to	has to	
4. have to	has to	

Test 5: *'im/*'em   (Do after Chapter 16.)

Listen to the short conversation. Which do you hear: *him* or *them*? Circle the correct word.

1. him	them
2. him	them
3. him	them
4. him	them
him	them
5. him	them
him	them

Test 6: *'n'/*'er   (Do after Chapter 18.)

Listen to the short conversation. Which do you hear: *and* or *or*? Circle the correct word.

1. and	or
2. and	or
3. and	or
and	or
4. and	or
5. and	or
and	or

Test 7: *er/*fer/*'er   (Do after Chapter 18.)

Listen to the short conversation. Which do you hear: *or, for,* or *her*? Circle the correct word.

1. or	for	her
or	for	her
2. or	for	her
3. or	for	her
or	for	her
4. or	for	her
or	for	her
5. or	for	her

Test 8: *Whaddaya   (Do after Chapter 22.)

Listen to the short conversation. Which do you hear: *What do you, What are you,* or *What have you?* Circle the correct words.

1. What do you	What are you	What have you
2. What do you	What are you	What have you
3. what do you	what are you	what have you
4. What do you	What are you	What have you
5. What do you	What are you	What have you

Test 9: *'ave/*'as/*'ad   (Do after Chapter 23.)

Listen to the short conversation. Which do you hear: *have, has,* or *had?* Circle the correct word.

1. have	has	had
2. have	has	had
have	has	had
3. have	has	had
have	has	had
4. have	has	had
have	has	had

Test 10: *shoulda/*shouldna   (Do after Chapter 24.)
*coulda/*couldna
*woulda/*wouldna

Listen to the short conversation. Which do you hear: *should have, shouldn't have; could have, couldn't have; would have* or *wouldn't have?* Circle the correct words.

1. should have	shouldn't have
should have	shouldn't have
2. could have	couldn't have
3. would have	wouldn't have
should have	shouldn't have
4. could have	couldn't have
would have	wouldn't have
5. could have	couldn't have

Test Yourself Tapescript

Test 1: Do *ya/Are *ya

Listen to the short conversation. Which do you hear: *Do you* or *Are you?* Circle the correct words.

1. MALE: Do you like the eggs?
    FEMALE: Oh, yeah!
2. MALE: Are you finished?
    FEMALE: Yeah.
3. MALE: Do you want anything else?
    FEMALE: No.
4. MALE: Do you want the check?
    FEMALE: The check?
5. MALE: Yeah. Are you paying by credit card?
    FEMALE: Uh, no. Cash.

Test 2: *wanna/*gonna

Listen to the short conversation. Which do you hear: *want to* or *going to?* Circle the correct words.

1. TEENAGER: I want to use your credit card.
2. MOM: You're not going to use my credit card.
3. TEENAGER: I'm not going to spend much.
4. MOM: You're not going to spend *anything*.
5. TEENAGER: I just want to buy a jacket. I don't want to spend a lot. Really.

Test 3: *kin/*kant

Listen to the short convrsation. Which do you hear: *can* or *can't?* Circle the correct word.

1. MALE #1:   Can you sing opera?
2. MALE #1:   You can't sing opera, can you?
3. MALE #2:   No, I can't, but I can dance.
4. MALE #1:   Can you tap dance?
5. MALE #2:   Well, no, I can't, but I can learn.

Test 4: *hafta/*hasta

Listen to the short conversation. Which do you hear: *have to* or *has to?* Circle the correct words.

1. FEMALE #1:   What do you have to do?
2. FEMALE #2:   I have to help my brother. He has to write a report.
3. FEMALE #1:   He has to write a report?
4. FEMALE #2:   Yes, and I have to help him.

Test 5: *'im/*'em

Listen to the short conversation. Which do you hear: *him* or *them?* Circle the correct word.

1. FEMALE: Tell him what you want.
2. MALE: I can't tell him. I need to tell the whole class.
3. FEMALE: Okay, tell them what you want.
4. MALE: I don't want to tell them now. I'll tell them later.
5. FEMALE: Oh, all right. Tell him when you tell all of them.

Test 6: *'n'/*er

Listen to the short conversation. Which do you hear: *and* **or** *or?* **Circle the correct word.**

1. MALE: I want some chips and dip for the party.
2. FEMALE: Do you want cheese or onion dip?
3. MALE: Onion dip. And how about some sandwiches and sodas?
4. FEMALE: Do you want turkey sandwiches or chicken?
5. MALE: Chicken. And I want them on wheat or rye bread.

Test 7: *er/*fer/*'er

Listen to the short conversation. Which do you hear: *or, for,* **or** *her?* **Circle the correct word.**

1. FEMALE: Do you want to go with her, or should I?
2. MALE: Does she want to go shopping, or does she want to go to a movie?
3. FEMALE: She wants to go shopping for an hour or two.
4. MALE: I'll go shopping with her. I'd like to do something for a few hours.
5. FEMALE: All right. I'll tell her.

Test 8: *Whaddaya

Listen to the short conversation. Which do you hear: *What do you, What are you,* **or** *What have you?* **Circle the correct words.**

1. MALE #1: What are you doing?
2. MALE #2: Nothing. What do you have in mind?
3. MALE #1: Well, what are you watching on TV?
4. MALE #2: It's almost 8:00 P.M. What do you think I'm watching?
5. MALE #1: I don't know. What have you decided to watch?

Test 9: *'ave/*'as/*'ad

Listen to the short conversation.

1. MALE #1: What have you done?
2. MALE #2: Nothing. I had just finished reading my book when I saw it.
   What has *she* done?
3. MALE #1: She's only three years old. What do you mean, "What has *she* done?"
   What have *you* done? You're supposed to be watching her.
4. MALE #2: What have *they* done? She had to draw on the *wall.* They didn't give her any paper.

Test 10: *shoulda/*shouldna
*coulda/*couldna
*woulda/*wouldna

Listen to the short conversation. Which do you hear: *should have, shouldn't have; could have, couldn't have; would have* **or** *wouldn't have?* **Circle the correct words.**

1. MALE: I should have just had coffee. I shouldn't have eaten those two pieces of pie and the rest of the cake.
2. FEMALE: You couldn't have eaten all of that!
3. MALE: Well, I did. I wouldn't have eaten the pie, but it was chocolate. I shouldn't have eaten the cake, too.
4. FEMALE: *I* couldn't have eaten all of that. I would have stopped after the pie.
5. MALE: I could have tried, but the cake was also chocolate.

Answer Key (Part 2, Practice)

1. How's Your Family? (*yer)

Practice, Page 3

1. your	3. you're	5. your	7. your	9. your	11. You're
2. You're	4. You're	6. your	8. your	10. Your	12. You're

2. Yours Is a Great Job! (*yers)

Practice, Page 6

1. yours	3. You're	5. Your	7. yours	9. Yours	11. Yours
2. Your	4. yours	6. Yours	8. Your	10. you're	

3. I Have the Perfect Car for You (*fer)

Practice, Page 9

1. for	4. You're	7. for	10. for	12. You're	14. for
2. For	5. for	8. Your	11. for	13. for	15. your
3. For	6. for	9. For			

4. Where Are the Bags of Chips? (*a)

Practice, Page 12

1. You're	4. of	7. of	10. your	13. of	15. of
2. your	5. of	8. for	11. of	14. of	16. for
3. of	6. of	9. of	12. for		

5. Do You Like the Internet? (*ya)

Practice, Page 15

1. your	4. you	7. You're	10. You're	13. of	15. you
2. you	5. your	8. you	11. You're	14. you	16. for
3. you	6. you	9. you	12. you		

6. Let's Go Shopping (*in')

Practice, Page 18

1. you	6. for	10. of	14. For	18. taking	22. you
2. looking	7. your	11. your	15. going	19. of	23. You're
3. for	8. you	12. looking	16. going	20. wearing	24. standing
4. you	9. you	13. for	17. you	21. for	25. of
5. looking					

7. What Are You Doing This Weekend? (*Whaddaya)

Practice, Page 21

1. what	6. you	10. you	14. yours	18. jumping	22. what
2. do	7. having	11. drinking	15. you	19. What	23. are
3. you	8. what	12. of	16. What	20. do	24. you
4. What	9. are	13. of	17. do	21. you	25. writing
5. do					

8. I Want to Have a Hamburger (*wanna)

Practice, Page 24

1 What	7. to	13. want	19. to	24. you	29. for
2. do	8. want	14. to	20. you	25. want	30. of
3. you	9. to	15. want	21. want	26. to	31. you
4. want	10. What	16. to	22. to	27. for	32. you
5. to	11. do	17. of	23. of	28. your	33. you
6. want	12. you	18. want			

9. We're Going to See "The Monster That Ate Cleveland" (*gonna)

Practice, Page 28

1. what	7. to	13. going	19. you	25. you	31. to
2. are	8. You	14. you	20. going	26. going	32. want
3. you	9. you're	15. want	21. to	27. to	33. to
4. going	10. of	16. to	22. of	28. want	34. your
5. to	11. going	17. What	23. want	29. to	35. want
6. going	12. to	18. are	24. to	30. going	36. to

10. Can You See the Stage? (*kin, *kant)

Practice, Page 31

1. Can	8. Can	14. What	20. Can	26. playing	32. can't
2. you	9. you	15. are	21. you	27. can't	33. Can
3. can't	10. going	16. you	22. you	28. you	34. you
4. of	11. to	17. saying	23. enjoying	29. can't	35. for
5. of	12. playing	18. can't	24. Can	30. want	36. can
6. Can	13. you	19. you	25. you	31. to	37. you
7. you					

11. What Can I Get You for Your Cold? (*git)

Practice, Page 34

1. you	7. going	13. you	19. get	24. can	29. get
2. doing	8. to	14. Can	20. for	25. get	30. you
3. get	9. You're	15. you	21. get	26. you	31. Can
4. Can	10. for	16. get	22. yours	27. for	32. you
5. get	11. what	17. can	23. for	28. can	33. get
6. you	12. do	18. you			

12. Take Bus 4 to Second Street (*ta)

Practice, Page 37

1. you	8. you	14. to	20. are	26. to	32. to
2. to	9. for	15. What	21. you	27. get	33. to
3. To	10. What	16. do	22. going	28. to	34. get
4. you	11. do	17. you	23. to	29. of	35. of
5. to	12. you	18. to	24. want	30. Your	36. to
6. get	13. want	19. What	25. to	31. to	37. to
7. Can					

13. I'm Going to Try to Find a Job (*da)

Practice, Page 40

1. going	7. to	13. of	19. want	25. to	31. to
2. to	8. to	14. to	20. to	26. of	32. you
3. go	9. want	15. your	21. to	27. you	33. want
4. to	10. to	16. to	22. to	28. want	34. to
5. to	11. go	17. for	23. Can	29. to	35. to
6. get	12. to	18. you	24. you	30. to	36. for

14. I've Got to Check Your Teeth (*gotta, *hafta, *hasta)

Practice, Page 43

1. got	8. you	15. has	21. can	27. to	33. got
2. to	9. You	16. to	22. have	28. have	34. to
3. has	10. have	17. you	23. to	29. to	35. has
4. to	11. to	18. has	24. to	30. to	36. to
5. going	12. You	19. to	25. to	31. got	37. got
6. to	13. going	20. to	26. have	32. to	38. to
7. to	14. to				

15. I Used to Be an Engineer for the Railroad (*useta, *supposta)

Practice, Page 46

1. You	10. to	19. you	27. changing	35. used	43. to
2. can't	11. You're	20. to	28. for	36. to	44. supposed
3. for	12. You're	21. used	29. to	37. for	45. to
4. You	13. supposed	22. to	30. you	38. for	46. for
5. can't	14. to	23. supposed	31. of	39. used	47. supposed
6. supposed	15. You	24. to	32. you	40. to	48. to
7. to	16. used	25. supposed	33. used	41. to	49. of
8. want	17. to	26. to	34. to	42. used	50. to
9. to	18. to				

16. What's the Fastest Way to Send His Packages? (*'e, *'is, *'im, *'er, *'em)

Practice, Page 50

1. want	11. have	21. her	30. them	39. your	48. them
2. to	12. to	22. have	31. her	40. he	49. his
3. to	13. get	23. to	32. her	41. get	50. he
4. you	14. them	24. get	33. you	42. them	51. can't
5. want	15. him	25. to	34. them	43. for	52. his
6. to	16. What	26. he	35. him	44. his	53. going
7. them	17. do	27. has	36. you	45. him	54. to
8. sending	18. you	28. to	37. them	46. he	55. to
9. them	19. to	29. get	38. to	47. get	56. You're
10. to	20. her				

17. We Arrive on Tuesday and Leave on Thursday (*'n')

Practice, Page 54

1. and	8. Can't	15. you	21. and	27. and	33. and
2. singing	9. you	16. And	22. yours	28. Can't	34. you
3. and	10. him	17. can	23. And	29. and	35. can
4. playing	11. to	18. for	24. Can	30. and	36. and
5. singing	12. to	19. and	25. and	31. of	37. can
6. and	13. him	20. for	26. can't	32. and	38. to
7. playing	14. can't				

18. Do You Want a Chocolate or Lemon Birthday Cake? (*er)

Practice, Page 58

1. you	10. What	19. to	28. you	37. and	46. supposed
2. want	11. do	20. can't	29. your	38. You	47. to
3. to	12. you	21. you	30. or	39. them	48. your
4. or	13. or	22. or	31. can	40. you	49. or
5. you	14. you	23. your	32. you	41. get	50. you
6. want	15. going	24. And	33. or	42. your	51. can
7. to	16. to	25. you	34. you	43. You	52. you
8. want	17. of	26. What	35. to	44. can	53. to
9. to	18. got	27. do	36. your	45. you're	

19. I Don't Know What Classes to Take (*donno)

Practice, Page 62

1. you	9. to	17. don't	24. thinking	31. your	38. to
2. doing	10. You're	18. know	25. don't	32. don't	39. you
3. don't	11. what	19. you	26. know	33. know	40. you
4. know	12. do	20. want	27. you	34. you're	41. can
5. can	13. you	21. to	28. can	35. thinking	42. you
6. you	14. want	22. used	29. you	36. you	43. don't
7. don't	15. to	23. to	30. to	37. have	44. know
8. know	16. you				

20. Can't You Find an Apartment? (*cha, *cher)

Practice, Page 65

1. you	9. you	17. you	25. want	32. to	39. want
2. to	10. you	18. to	26. to	33. want	40. to
3. you	11. what	19. for	27. at	34. to	41. what
4. to	12. you're	20. of	28. your	35. aren't	42. you're
5. you	13. looking	21. you	29. and	36. you	43. looking
6. you	14. got	22. What	30. You're	37. don't	44. for
7. want	15. to	23. you're	31. going	38. know	45. or
8. to	16. don't	24. saying			

21. Could You Check My Sink? (*ja, *jer)

Practice, Page 68

1. your	8. your	15. to	22. You	28. Did	34. going
2. you	9. you	16. and	23. have	29. you	35. to
3. your	10. your	17. you	24. to	30. your	36. for
4. going	11. them	18. your	25. Can't	31. you	37. and
5. to	12. or	19. Would	26. you	32. you	38. Could
6. have	13. Your	20. you	27. them	33. can	39. you
7. to	14. have	21. to			

22. Who Have You Asked to Fly the Plane? (*'ave, *'as, *'ad)

Practice, Page 72

1. What	10. you	19. going	28. to	37. had	46. have
2. are	11. doing	20. to	29. has	38. don't	47. you
3. you	12. jogging	21. You	30. he	39. know	48. to
4. doing	13. playing	22. used	31. to	40. you	49. has
5. have	14. and	23. to	32. he	41. he	50. taking
6. you	15. to	24. have	33. had	42. to	51. her
7. have	16. have	25. to	34. you	43. has	52. you
8. what	17. you	26. have	35. and	44. his	53. want
9. have	18. to	27. you	36. he	45. to	54. to

23. Could I Have an Appointment with Dr. Okamoto? (*'ave, *'as, *'ad)

Practice, Page 76

1. you	11. to	20. you	29. you	38. He	47. hasn't
2. have	12. your	21. your	30. You're	39. had	48. for
3. had	13. to	22. for	31. saying	40. to	49. for
4. your	14. you	23. have	32. have	41. you	50. You're
5. want	15. to	24. can't	33. of	42. have	51. going
6. to	16. have	25. you	34. did	43. for	52. to
7. to	17. of	26. had	35. you	44. He	53. have
8. your	18. to	27. get	36. your	45. has	54. to
9. haven't	19. Can	28. have	37. Playing	46. He	55. for
10. listening					

24. We Should Have Taken a Left (*shoulda, *coulda, *woulda, *musta, *maya, *mighta, *shouldna, *couldna, *wouldna)

Practice, Page 80

1. should	11. have	21. may	31. have	40. your	49. of
2. have	12. must	22. have	32. looking	41. you	50. for
3. couldn't	13. have	23. or	33. for	42. must	51. your
4. have	14. could	24. shouldn't	34. You	43. have	52. wouldn't
5. Didn't	15. have	25. have	35. should	44. and	53. have
6. you	16. don't	26. you	36. have	45. couldn't	54. and
7. of	17. know	27. yelling	37. you	46. have	55. you
8. to	18. to	28. Can	38. would	47. might	56. hadn't
9. had	19. must	29. you	39. have	48. have	57. You
10. would	20. have	30. might			

25. What Are You Doing to My Hair? (*Whatcha)

Practice, Page 84

1. what	11. to	20. doing	29. You're	38. to	47. cutting
2. are	12. to	21. you	30. going	39. to	48. You
3. you	13. you're	22. or	31. to	40. got	49. to
4. doing	14. and	23. What	32. don't	41. to	50. what
5. doing	15. you	24. are	33. know	42. them	51. have
6. what	16. you	25. you	34. What	43. What	52. you
7. you	17. you	26. taking	35. are	44. are	53. to
8. to	18. what	27. or	36. you	45. you	54. to
9. cutting	19. you're	28. you	37. going	46. doing	55. of
10. your					

26. Give Me a Paintbrush (*lemme, *gimme)

Practice, Page 88

1. want	10. to	19. Give	28. Give	37. me	45. have
2. to	11. You	20. me	29. me	38. You're	46. you
3. you	12. don't	21. get	30. of	39. Let	47. your
4. to	13. know	22. want	31. Give	40. me	48. of
5. to	14. Let	23. to	32. me	41. yours	49. Let
6. to	15. me	24. get	33. get	42. You	50. me
7. to	16. You	25. Let	34. give	43. you	51. used
8. of	17. Give	26. me	35. me	44. What	52. to
9. used	18. me	27. you	36. Let		

27. I Couldn't Take the Test Because I Was Sick (*'bout, *'cause, *c'mon)

Practice, Page 92

1. you	10. to	19. to	28. You're	36. to	44. because
2. going	11. you	20. get	29. working	37. come	45. got
3. have	12. About	21. want	30. for	38. on	46. to
4. to	13. you	22. to	31. about	39. going	47. get
5. because	14. have	23. to	32. get	40. to	48. you
6. of	15. to	24. have	33. have	41. got	49. About
7. Come	16. get	25. have	34. to	42. to	50. you
8. on	17. because	26. to	35. have	43. to	51. you
9. have	18. want	27. because			

28. Been to the Circus Lately? (Deletions of Words in Questions)

Practice, Page 96

1. want	10. Do	18. know	26. to	34. Do	42. You
2. you	11. you	19. Would	27. Come	35. you	43. going
3. to	12. Want	20. you	28. on	36. Know	44. to
4. going	13. to	21. Like	29. you	37. want	45. Do
5. to	14. You	22. to	30. to	38. to	46. you
6. to	15. don't	23. have	31. them	39. want	47. Want
7. meet	16. you	24. you	32. to	40. to	48. to
8. you	17. don't	25. seen	33. him	41. Are	49. you
9. and					

29. Where Are Your Extra-Large Hats? (Unusual Contractions)

Practice, Page 100

1. For	12. Where	23. where	34. are	45. will	56. have
2. To	13. are	24. will	35. you	46. have	57. to
3. to	14. your	25. Let	36. looking	47. to	58. to
4. you	15. going	26. me	37. Where	48. to	59. you
5. Where	16. to	27. you	38. will	49. to	60. to
6. will	17. have	28. to	39. them	50. them	61. can
7. connect	18. to	29. you	40. have	51. talking	62. you
8. you	19. you	30. Why	41. to	52. to	63. Your
9. to	20. to	31. are	42. you	53. your	64. to
10. Can	21. Can	32. your	43. to	54. What	65. can't
11. you	22. you	33. What	44. Why	55. will	

30. When Will Your TV Program Be Over? (Unusual Contractions)

Practice, Page 104

1. When	10. want	19. of	27. supposed	35. kidding	43. will
2. are	11. to	20. talking	28. to	36. have	44. can't
3. you	12. What	21. about	29. You	37. to	45. got
4. going	13. do	22. You	30. have	38. How	46. to
5. to	14. you	23. supposed	31. you	39. will	47. Have
6. your	15. want	24. to	32. Who	40. got	48. you
7. watching	16. to	25. How	33. are	41. to	49. Seen
8. When	17. going	26. are	34. you	42. Who	50. of
9. will	18. to				

Test Yourself Answer Key

Test 1: Do *ya/Are *ya

1. Do you
2. Are you
3. Do you
4. Do you
5. Are you

Test 2: *wanna/*gonna

1. want to
2. going to
3. going to
4. going to
5. want to
   want to

Test 3: *kin/*kant

1. Can
2. can't
   can
3. can't
   can
4. Can
5. can't
   can

Test 4: *hafta/*hasta

1. have to
2. have to
   has to
3. has to
4. have to

Test 5: *'im/*'em

1. him
2. him
3. them
4. them
   them
5. him
   them

Test 6: *'n'/*er

1. and
2. or
3. And
   and
4. or
5. And
   or

Test 7: *er/*fer/*'er

1. her
   or
2. or
3. for
   or
4. her
   for
5. her

Test 8: *Whaddaya

1. What are you
2. What do you
3. What are you
4. What do you
5. What have you

Test 9: *'ave/*'as/*'ad

1. have
2. had
   has
3. has
   have
4. have
   had

Test 10: *shoulda/*shouldna
*coulda/*couldna
*woulda/*wouldna

1. should have
   shouldn't have
2. couldn't have
3. wouldn't have
   shouldn't have
4. couldn't have
   would have
5. could have

Alternate Levels of Reductions

The pronunciation levels will be shown as Levels 1, 2, 3, and 4.

Example:

Chapter	Level 1: *Slowest*	Level 2: *Slow*	Level 3: *Faster*	Level 4: *Fastest*
9	going to + verb	going *ta	*gonna	*'onna (only after "I'm")

In my research, which consisted of recordings of unscripted speech by highly educated native English speakers, Level 1 speech occurred 8 times, Level 2 reductions occurred 47 times, and Level 3 reductions occurred 258 times. Therefore, when there is more than one level of reduction possible, *Whaddaya Say?*, *Second Edition*, focuses on Level 3 reductions, which are the most common.

Chapter	Level 1	Level 2	Level 3	Level 4
7	What do you What do {we / they} What are you	*Whadda you *Wha do {we / they} *What're *ya	*Whaddaya *Whadda *Whaddaya	
8	want to	want *ta	*wanna	
9	going to + verb	going *ta	*gonna	*'onna (only after "I'm")
13	*to* after vowel sound	*ta	*da	
14	got to have to haf to has to	got *ta have *ta has *ta	gotta *hafta *hasta	 *'afta *'asta
15	used to supposed to	used *ta supposed *ta	*useta *supposta	 *s'posta
20	/t/ + you /t/+ your, you're	*ya *chou *yer	*cha *cher	
21	/d/ + you /d/ + your	*ya *jou *yer	*ja *jer	
22	What have you What have {we / they}	What *'ave you What *'ave	What *of you What *of	*Whaddaya *Whadda
23	Subject + have	*'ave	*of	
24	modals + have + past participle	should *of could *of (etc.)	*shoulda *coulda (etc.)	
25	What are you	What *chou	*Whacha	